Constanze Mozart
An Unimportant Woman

Studies in Austrian Literature, Culture, and Thought

Translation Series

Renate Welsh

Constanze Mozart
An Unimportant Woman

Preface by Gerhard Weiss

Translated and with an Afterword

by Beth Bjorklund

ARIADNE PRESS
Riverside, California

...reciation to the Austrian Cultural
...ramt – Kunst, Vienna for their
... this book.

... German
Constanze Mozart: Eine unbedeutende Frau
© 1990 by Esslinger Edition J & V
Verlag J.F. Schreiber GmbH
P.O. Box 285
D-73703 Esslingen, Germany

Library of Congress Cataloging-in-Publication Data

Welsh, Renate, 1937-
    [Constanze Mozart. English]
    Constanze Mozart : an unimportant woman / Renate Welsh ; preface
by Gerhard Weiss ; translated and with an afterword by Beth Bjorklund.
        p.   cm. -- (Studies in Austrian literature, culture, and
thought. Translation series)
    Summary: Fifty years after the death of her husband, Wolfgang
Amadeus Mozart, Constanze reflects on her long life.
    ISBN 0-57241-036-1
    1. Mozart, Constanze, 1763-1842--Juvenile fiction. 2. Mozart,
Wolfgang Amadeus, 1756-1791--Juvenile fiction. [1. Mozart,
Constanze, 1763-1842--Fiction. 2. Mozart, Wolfgang Amadeus, 1756
-1791--Fiction. 3. Old age--Fiction. 4. Austria--Fiction.]
    I. Bjorklund, Beth. II. Title. III. Series
PZ7.W46855Co   1997
[Fic]--dc21   97-3449
                                                      CIP
                                                       AC

Cover Design:
Art Director, Designer: George McGinnis
Illustration: Gesellschaft der Musikfreunde, Vienna

Copyright ©1997
by Ariadne Press
270 Goins Court
Riverside, CA 92507

Preface

"A certain Constanze Weber has joined the ranks of the immortals. To be sure, nobody could be more surprised about this fact than she herself would have been during the period of her marriage. Granted, she had still experienced Mozart's becoming famous, had still benefited from its financial implications, which she had furthered to the best of her ability, but the genius of her husband she really had never fully grasped, not even after his death, when others began to make her aware of the aura of his reputation."[1]

Constanze von Nissen, Widow Mozart, née Weber, is a central figure in the life of Mozart and in the legends that have evolved after the great composer's death. Whatever we know about Constanze comes almost entirely from secondary sources: from Mozart's letters to her or about her, from letters of Mozart's father and sister (neither of whom liked her), and from comments and reports of those who knew her or simply speculated about her. Constanze's own letters to Wolfgang and there must have been many, considering how often he acknowledges their receipt – are lost. There are a few petitions for a widow's pension, written after the composer's death, and there are some business-related and personal notes from her later years.[2] One of the more favorable portraits of the aging Constanze can be found in the 1829 diaries of Vincent and Mary Novello who, as Mozart admirers, had visited and interviewed the composer's widow at her Nonnberg residence in Salzburg.[3]

Based, as it were, on flimsy anecdotal evidence, Constanze's image in history has been a shaky one. In the eyes of many, especially German, musicologists, she is "perhaps the most unpopular woman in music history."[4] She is accused of having been a shallow, silly, sensuous woman who in no way understood the musical genius of her husband. She is charged with having been a hypochondriac who wasted Mozart's meager resources on expensive cures, a woman who encouraged the composer's "scatterbrained, if not absolutely dissolute, life,"[5] a widow who did not attend her husband's funeral, who failed to order a marker for his grave, and then, not until seventeen years after his death, made her one and only feeble attempt to visit Mozart's final resting place.[6] She has been accused of marketing the memory of Mozart in her later years, hypocritically becoming the "pious keeper of his shrine." In Peter Shaffer's play *Amadeus* we hear Constanze speak (reverentially) "A sweeter-tongued man never lived. In ten years of blissful marriage I never heard him utter a single coarse or conceited word. The purity of his life is reflected absolutely in the purity of his music!..[more briskly]. In selling his manuscripts I charge by the ink. So many notes, so many schillings."[7] The film version of Shaffer's play, a world-wide success, has further contributed to this highly critical view of Mozart's Constanze.

Constanze certainly was no angel. She was a very ordinary woman of limited beauty and some musical talent. She was twenty years old when Mozart married her, and twenty-eight when he died. She came from a lower-middle-class home of limited financial means, one of six children of Fridolin and Caecilia Weber. Her father earned a pittance as a bass singer, violinist and theater prompter. Her mother – by all accounts – was an extremely unpleasant woman. Mozart had originally fallen in love with Constanze's older sister Aloysia, a talented singer who later had leading roles in a number of Mozart's operas. When Aloysia spurned Mozart's attentions, he began to court Constanze. She was – and she knew it – his "second choice." Nevertheless, she seems to have genuinely loved him, and – unless his letters deceive us – he also loved her, indeed was infatuated with her.

But Constanze had married Mozart the man, not Mozart the genius. It was Mozart the private person who had attracted her, "a short slim man who made her laugh," and "this pale man with sallow complexion was no fairy-tale prince" (Renate Welsh). The world may admire him as the greatest composer alive – she had to do his laundry, she had to nurse him in his sickness, she had to be with the children during the many and long periods of his absence, and she had to manage a household with always insufficient means. She had no identity of her own – no voice of her own. She was known as Mozart's wife, and later his widow – even after she had remarried, and her second husband had also passed away. That was her role in life. To be sure, she benefited from the Mozart name, especially in her older age. There were financial advantages, and a certain degree of fame. Had she only been married to George Nicolaus Nissen (her second husband), nobody would have remembered her. On the other hand, her "fame" was also coupled with notoriety – she had become an easy target for those who needed a scapegoat for everything that had gone wrong in Mozart's life.

History has seen Constanze only through the eyes of others. But, she cannot only be "Frau Mozart." Behind the name, there must be hiding a genuine human being, a human being who is trying to cope with all the difficulties of life. To speculate what this human being might really have been like as a person has been Renate Welsh's task in the subsequent portions of this book. It is fiction, to be sure, but fiction based on careful research and on profound human understanding. Renate Welsh, well-known and respected as a writer of books for children and young people, has often chosen "outsiders" as protagonists for her stories, and she sees in Constanze such an outsider, a person who is marked for life, because in her youth she had been married for eight years to a man whose greatness she did not even comprehend.[8] Now, in her old age – in our book she is seventy-nine – Constanze reflects on her long life, slowly and haltingly, because as Welsh says: "It was simply too late when

Constanze had first learned to think. One needs words for thinking, not just the everyday words that she had at her command." However, it is precisely the intensity of her "simple language" that underscores the humanness of this "unimportant" person. She had no fancy words, no great music to express her feelings. Her Requiem consists of memories, of reflections, of becoming herself. Renate Welsh removes the labels that contemporaries and later generations have put on Constanze Mozart, and what is left is a truly human being.

Beth Bjorklund, a scholar well versed in Austrian literature and culture, has given us a close and sensitive translation of Renate Welsh's text. The language of Constanze's Austria has not been artificially recreated. Welsh writes a modern idiom of impeccable directness, void of any sentimentality. Bjorklund has captured the effectiveness of this language through her translation. Was Constanze Weber-Mozart-Nissen really just an "unimportant woman"? The readers will have to find out for themselves, because here the book begins...

Gerhard Weiss
University of Minnesota

vi

Notes

1. Wolfgang Hildesheimer, *Mozart*. Frankfurt am Main: Suhrkamp, 1977, p. 261.Translation mine.

2. For more details, see Arthur Schurig, *Konstanze Mozart. Briefe, Aufzeichnungen, Dokumente 1782-1842*.Dresden, 1922.

3. Nerina Medici and Rosemary Hughes, *A Mozart Pilgrimage: Being the Travel Diaries of Vincent and Mary Novello in the year 1829*. London: Novello and Co., 1955.

4. H. C. Robbins Landon, *1791: Mozart's Last Year*. New York: Schirmer Books, 1988. p.182.

5. Ibid., p.182.

6. Francis Carr, *Mozart and Constanze*. London: John Murray, Ltd., 1983. p.165.

7. Peter Shaffer, *Amadeus*. New York: Harper & Row, 1981. p. 92.

8. Interview with Renate Welsh, conducted by Karin Sollat, in: "Ich kann dir keine Antwort geben, aber steh zu deinen Fragen." Laudatio, Österreichischer Würdigungspreis für Kinder- und Jugendliteratur, 1992, p. 3.

Constanze von Nissen,
Mozart's widow,
fifty years after Mozart's death,
as her own long life
was drawing to a close –
Let's imagine . . .

An old woman was looking out at the rain. Big drops splashed on the cobblestones, forming bubbles before they burst and spattered. The large square was empty.

There in the middle, that was where the monument would be.

It would already be there if things had gone as they should have. But the Roman mosaics had come in between. Why did they have to be discovered? Exactly on this spot, as the foundation was being excavated. What on earth were Roman mosaics doing here? As if there were not enough old stones in the world anyway.

The bronze statue had been cast in May 1841 in the Royal Munich Foundry. In the presence of her Royal Highness the Duchess Sophia and numerous spectators. Constanze herself had not yet seen the statue. Everyone else had, but not she. They could, of course, get away with treating a member of the Weber family like that.

The middle of the square was dug up, looked as if it had been plowed. They were acting as if they had all the time in the world. But if they did not hurry it would soon be too late, too late for her anyway.

Sometimes she felt a coldness creeping into her joints. Extra blankets or a bed warmer full of glowing coals were no help then, nor were warm scarves or hot tea. On days like today when it was raining, that was not particularly surprising; but it also happened on days when the sun beat down on the city. The coldness brought with it anxiety, a strangling kind of fear. Even praying could not ward it off.

"Sophie!"[1]

Her sister did not come. Had apparently tuned out again. Sophie's hearing was not really any worse than her own, she surmised. Sophie was simply lazy on occasion. The spoiled baby of the family. Whereas, in fact, she had every reason to be thankful.

"Sophie!"

The answer was inaudible. There were shuffling footsteps in one of the back rooms.

She could at least lift her feet a little when she walked.

Now Sophie was standing in front of her, her face turned toward the window. She certainly had a lot of wrinkles. Loose, flabby skin over sunken cheeks.

"Just look at that down there, Sophie. They're gone again today."

"It's pouring down rain."

"But they don't work when the sun is shining either."

"They were working yesterday."

"If they don't hurry up it will be too late."

"Oh, come on. Lunch will be ready soon."

"Food is all you ever think about."

"Somebody has to."

"Do you think it'll stop raining?"

"Maybe. A shower doesn't last long. Luise[2] wants to take the afternoon off. It's her mother's nameday."

"She has a lot of namedays."

"Last time it was her sister's, and that was four months ago, if not five."

"Carl[3] could at least write sometime."

"Do you want a cup of tea?"

"I'd rather have coffee."

"Now, before lunch?"

"Yes, now, before lunch."

How reproachful she seemed as she walked out. A cup of coffee was really not too much to ask for. Sophie was acting as if she were the one who had to pay for it.

Constanze leaned back. The time was past when she had to watch every penny. Now she could afford more coffee than she could drink in a whole lifetime.

Her eyes wandered around the room, then fixed on the wooden inlay of a dresser. How one swirl engaged another. A nice piece of furniture, really nice. But Luise ought to rub it again with beeswax. And thoroughly polish it. Wood dries out and can crack. It gets tiny cracks, as fine as a hair.

"Yes," she murmured. "You'd be surprised, would-n't you, Mister Deputy Music Director, how well I'm living now." With a view of the square in its entire expanse, not just the narrow confines of Getreide Street.

"What did you say," Sophie called from the kitchen.

"Nothing."

"But you did say something!"

"No."

That was none of her business. That was between her and her father-in-law, Johann Georg Leopold Mozart.[4] Dear old father. Très cher père. The father who was "second only to God."

She had never been good enough for him. She, a Weber woman. If only he could see her now!

He had not given her a single thing at the time of her first visit in Salzburg. No ring, no snuffbox, no purse, no buckle, nothing, not even a dress pin. He showed her the memorabilia that "his Wolfie" had received as a *Wunderkind*; that part of it anyway that had not been sold to cover travel expenses. He also showed her the pictures and miniatures. But he never said, "As his wife, you too should have some of the gifts." He acted as if the things belonged to him, Mozart's father. Talked about the sacrifices he had made for the education of his children. Mozart himself was irritated by it. But to say something – oh, no, never – not against his father.

Then when they got back to their home in Vienna, in the summer of 1783, little Raimund[5] was already dead and buried.

Raimund had been the biggest of her babies. His birth had caused her the most difficulty. Mozart had come into her bedroom again and again. His eyes filled with tears, he stroked her sweaty face until the midwife threw him out. Then when the child was finally born, Mozart took him in his arms and danced around with him. The midwife scolded him and threw up her hands at such foolishness.

What did Raimund look like?

Was he the one with all that dark hair? Or was that Johannes,[6] the third child? She could not remember. Two months, one month – their lives were so short. How was she supposed to remember, since she always got pregnant again right away. Always had swollen legs, was always heavy and tired.

"Here's the coffee."

"Aren't you having any?"

"I'm busy."

"You think you're so important."

Contanze picked up the cup, inhaled the aroma. It was not raining so hard anymore. A sparrow was sitting on the window casing. It chirped loudly, shaking itself.

Constanze gripped the armrests of her chair with both hands, pressed against them and then let up. Transferring as much of her weight as possible to her hands, she managed to stand up.

Her legs held the weight. That was a success. She reached for the cane that was leaned up against the table. The handle felt good, firm and round.

On her way through the room she glanced in the mirror. Her face looked unfamiliar.

Where did that hair on her chin come from, the long black one? Her mother had had facial hair like that. She took the hair between her thumb and forefinger, pulled, but could not get a grip on it. She tried again and again. Her thumbnail dug into the skin of her forefinger, left a red half-moon. She became impatient and frustrated.

She did not want to ask Sophie to pluck the hair. Even if Sophie did not say anything, she would still be thinking, "just like our dear old mother." There! A tiny sting. She held the hair in her hand, rolled it together, flicked it away, and immediately felt irritated. She should have burned it. But if she looked for it now on the floor, Sophie would probably come in and bombard her with questions. Besides, what did she care about a hair?

Outside a pickax was clinking against a stone. The workmen were back.

Luise brought in the soup.

Constanze propped herself up with both arms on the desk and stared at the open drawer.

What was she looking for? Something that was in this drawer, otherwise she would not have opened it. She was not stupid. Wowi's[7] letters were in the left front corner, next to those from Carl. Two small piles. As much as half a year sometimes passed between two letters. Mozart had written to his father at least twice a week, no matter how busy he was.

But her boys?

She sighed. She knew so little of her sons, those distant grown men, as distant from each other as they were from her. Of course, they had not grown up together either. The portrait showed them with their arms around each other and holding hands. It had been etched and reproduced as "A Portrait of Brotherly Love." By whom, actually? Wowi was six years old at the time, and as she thought about him today the portrait intruded on her memory. She had not found it particularly successful at the time when the portraitist was doing the finishing touches. She had complained about one thing or another. But Wowi's gaze which, while turned to his brother, looked right at the viewer, was well done, also the hint of a smile on his face. He was always aware of it when people were looking at him.

How his eyes gleamed, how red his lips and cheeks were when he stood on a table in Prague and sang "The birdcatcher, that's me, Always happy as can be." Everyone was moved. She clearly recalled how she groped for a handkerchief, and Wowi smiled. He had the same sort of smile when she scolded him. It drove her crazy, that smile; as if he knew something she did not, as if he could see through her. He had smiled like that too over his breakfast milk the morning after her first night with Nissen.[8] She felt powerless, became angry, yelled at him when he dribbled on the tablecloth. It took a quiet nod from Nissen to bring her back to her senses.

People had reproached her for having the little boy perform for money. They should talk! What should she have done at the time, with only a measly widow's pension for two small children and all the bills. There had been absolutely no one in the whole world to whom she could have turned, until Nissen became her gentleman lodger. No one had faulted father Mozart for traveling halfway around the world with his two small children. He was not blamed, of course not. Only she.

What had people *not* reproached her for, openly or secretly, often as innuendo in a memorial in honor of

Mozart's genius.

But it was not the genius she had married.

She had married a short slim man who made her laugh. And God knows there had been precious little reason to laugh in her life until the day that young Mozart, the recently dismissed chief organist and concert master at the Prince-Archbishopric court, rented a room at her mother's house. The musician who could not sit still for a minute; who played on every free surface, treating every table top and windowsill like a mute keyboard; who fidgeted when he talked; who turned sounds and words around and made faces; from whom you never knew what to expect. This pale man with his sallow complexion was no fairy-tale prince. She had imagined the man of her dreams to be different. He would be taller, worthier; someone she could show off, and who would make other women jealous of her; someone who would take her away from the cramped quarters, the quarreling, the constant money problems; who would tell her that she, and only she, not Aloysia,[9] her big sister, was the most beautiful and also the most talented woman in the world; and who would say it until she herself could believe it. But Mozart was there, and they laughed together and were silly. Somehow, too, there was still a slight touch of residual sympathy from the time when Aloysia treated him so badly in Mannheim; no, that must have been in Munich. Aloysia, dizzy from her first triumphs as a prima donna, Mozart wearing black mourning crepe on the gold buttons of his red jacket, commemorating the death of his mother. Her sister had been heartless, thinking only of her own advantage, her own career. And then later, after she realized what she had lost, she had the gall to claim that Mozart had loved only her his whole life long. What did she know! Nothing. Absolutely nothing.

Constanze reached for her small gold watch, the watch that Mozart had given her when they became engaged. She breathed on it, rubbed it smooth on her dress, and held the watch in the palms of her hands.

She liked his music; but it was the man, not the music that she loved, the man who made her laugh. She could not say exactly when it was that she fell in love. It had come on quite imperceptibly, a laughing, giggling, tittering love without pining and yearning. Maybe it would not even have turned into love if her mother had not meddled, with her prohibitions and stipulations. Her mother, who, with her hair hanging down, used to get loud after her third glass of wine.

Constanze crossed herself.

One should not say bad things about the dead. Or even think anything bad. But still, it was true. For weeks her mother had looked on approvingly; had left her daughter alone in a room with Mozart; had walked behind with Sophie when they went out for a stroll; had sent Constanze to Mozart with a cup of coffee or a glass of lemonade; had laughed at his jokes and supported him in his anger at the Archbishop.[10] And then suddenly, overnight, he was an arch-scoundrel, a villain, a seducer, and her mother ranted and raved. The situation in her house at Petersplatz, "In the Eye of God,"[11] became increasingly intolerable, and Constanze cried herself to sleep almost every night. Leopold Mozart, in a letter to his son, called her mother a "*seductress of youth*." He wrote that one should hang a sign like that around her neck; she should be placed in irons and made to sweep the streets. She and Thorwart,[12] the guardian, that repulsive schemer. It was not until much later, however, that Constanze got to see that letter. And what if she had known about it earlier?

The difficulties only drew her and Mozart more closely together. Was it the very resistance that caused the infatuation to turn into love? By that time it was already past the point of no return. Mozart had already nested in her heart, and she knew how his insistent tenderness made her dizzy. She got goose bumps even where people do not get goose bumps, and she felt the blood throbbing in her ears and in her breasts.

But that is really not appropriate for an old woman, murmured Constanze. One should not even think about things like that. Not about the letters either, his letters, she admonished herself, and at the same time her fingers reached for the ribbon that was wrapped around the bundle. "1791 Letters"[13] was printed on it in Nissen's careful handwriting. She could not untie the knot, which, as she pulled and twisted, only became tighter. Finally, she took a small pair of scissors and cut the ribbon. The paper rustled in her hands.

Fifty years, my God, fifty years.

Her feet hurt, and the light would be better too in the armchair by the window; but she remained standing, her upper body tilted slightly back. She read a line here and another one there. No, not the begging letters to Puchberg,[14] she did not want to be reminded of them. It was not her baths in the expensive spas that made the constant loans necessary, really not. And if anybody claimed that she went there only to enjoy the pleasures of the resort and to be escorted around, that was a blatant lie. How could a person even go to the hall and dance with such a heavy body, on such swollen feet, racked with nausea?

She was reputed to be a pleasure seeker; rumor had it she was a bad housewife and completely unreasonable. But would it have been better if she had told Mozart that she did not share his eternally renewed hopes for the success of an opera, a commission, an academy, a decent job? Would they have preferred that?

Lots of people found fault – but no one ever helped. They patronized others, the Salieris,[15] the Dittersdorfs,[16] and their ilk. Puchberg had not spoken against her, nor had he insisted on prompt repayment of the money he had loaned Mozart. How much was it? A large sum in any event. She had paid it all back eventually, as she could, down to the last penny. Alright, so he had to remind her about it occasionally. But in the meantime years had passed, and Puchberg was very courteous, very obliging.

It was the others who spread the dirt.

She did not want to think about it. What was the point? What good would it do? Whom would it serve?

Here, that is what she was looking for: "*Ma très*

chère Épouse!"

The handwriting was so hard to read. He had written hurriedly, always in a hurry, often writing while getting ready to go out. And her eyes were not so good as they used to be.

"I have this moment received your letter, which has given me extraordinary pleasure. I am now longing for a second one to tell me how the baths are affecting you. I too am sorry not to have been present yesterday at your fine concert, not on account of the music, but because I should have been so happy to be with you.... Do not forget my warnings about the morning and evening air and about bathing too long.... Adieu. I kiss you two thousand times in thought and am ever

your Mozart

PS – Perhaps after all it would be well to give Carl a little rhubarb. Why did you not send me that long letter? Here is a letter for him – I should like to have an answer. Catch – Catch – bis -bis – bs – bs – kisses are flying about for you – bs – why, another one is staggering after the rest!

I have this moment received your second letter. Beware of the baths! And do sleep more – and not so irregularly, or I shall worry – I am a little anxious as it is.
Adieu."

It was in June '91 when he wrote that, after eight years of marriage, a month before Wowi's birth and half a year before his death.

How concerned he had been about her in each pregnancy, every illness. When she was so sick, two – or three – months before poor little Anna[17] was born, he suffered more than she. He did not even compose anything then, which he otherwise did all the time, often even producing the most cheerful melodies when he was the saddest.

He loved her.

People could say what they wanted. Let them talk.

He was happy with her, even during the years when so many hopes and plans were dashed.

She read a sentence here, a phrase there. Disconnected sentences, and she heard him speaking as she read.

But where was the part she was looking for? Perhaps in a different year? Of course, that letter had been from Dresden. Two years earlier. She took out the packet from 1789. A letter to Hofdemel.[18] He committed suicide shortly after Mozart's death; and before that he had seriously injured his pregnant wife. A sad story. Some people maintained that Mozart was the father of the child. Terrible, what people say; and you cannot defend yourself against it. Better not to think about it at all.

Here: "*Dearest little wife, if only I had a letter from you! If I were to tell you all the things I do with your dear portrait, I think that you would often laugh. For instance, when I take it out of its case, I say, 'Good-day, Stanzerl! – Good-day, little rascal, pussy-pussy, little turned-up nose, little bagatelle, Schluck und Druck', and when I put it away again, I let it slip in very slowly, saying all the time, 'Nu – Nu – Nu – Nu!' with the peculiar* emphasis *which this word so full of meaning demands, and then just at the last, quickly, 'Good night, little mouse, sleep well'. Well, I have been writing something very foolish (to the world at all events); but to us who love each other so dearly, it is not foolish at all. Today is the sixth day since I left you and by Heaven! it seems a year. I expect you will have some difficulty here and there in reading my letter, because I am writing in a hurry and therefore rather badly. Adieu, my only love! The carriage is waiting. This time I do not say: 'Hurrah – the carriage has come at last', but 'male' [Confound it!]. Farewell, and love me for ever as I love you. I kiss you a million times most lovingly and am ever your husband who loves you tenderly.*

W. A. Mozart"

The trip had been in vain. One of many failed trips. He wrote from Berlin:

"My darling little wife, when I return you must be more delighted with having me back than with the money I shall bring. A hundred friedrichs d'or are not nine hundred gulden but seven hundred – at least that is what they have told me here. Secondly, Lichnowsky[19] (as he was in a hurry) left me here, and so I have had to pay for my keep in Potsdam, which is an expensive place. Thirdly, I had to lend him a hundred gulden, as his purse was getting empty. I could not well refuse him: you will know why. Fourthly, my concert at Leipzig was a failure, as I always said it would be, so I had a journey of sixty-four miles there and back almost for nothing. Lichnowsky alone is to blame for this, for he

*gave me no peace but insisted on my returning to
Leipzig. I shall tell you more about this when we meet.
But (1) if I gave a concert here I should not make much
out of it and (2) the King would not care for me to give
one. So you must just be satisfied as I am with this, that I
am fortunate enough to be enjoying the King's favour.
What I have just written to you is for ourselves alone.
On Thursday, the 28th, I shall leave for Dresden, where
I shall spend the night. On June 1st I intend to sleep in
Prague, and on the 4th – the 4th – with my darling little
wife. Arrange your dear sweet nest very daintily, for my
little fellow deserves it indeed, he has really behaved
himself very well and is only longing to possess your
sweetest....[20] Just picture to yourself that rascal; as I
write he crawls on to the table and looks at me
questioningly. I, however, box his ears properly – but
the rogue is simply ... and now the knave burns only
more fiercely and can hardly be restrained."*

Her cheeks became flushed. After all these years.
Hurriedly she read on:

*"Surely, you will drive out to the first post-stage to
meet me? I shall get there at noon on the 4th. I hope
that Hofer,[21] whom I embrace a thousand times, will be
with you. If Herr and Frau von Puchberg drive out with
you too, then all the friends I want to see will be
together. Don't forget to bring our Carl. But the most
important thing of all is that you should have with you
someone you can rely on (Satmann[22] or someone else),
who can drive off to the customs in my carriage with my
luggage, so that I may not have to face that unnecessary*

*seccatura, but can drive home with all you dear people.
Now remember this.*

*Well, adieu. I kiss you millions of times and am
ever your most faithful husband*

W. A. Mozart"

That was Mozart all over. Amidst the most passionate
feeling an outbreak of sobriety or a switch to a different
mood, precisely the opposite. That was confusing for
anyone who knew him. It was different in his music,
there he always struck the right balance.

"Balance" was one of Nissen's favorite words. She
had learned it from him. When someone said "balance"
or "restraint," she automatically thought of Nissen, and
gratefully so. Mozart's volatile nature: for her it was like
being forced to jump from cliff to cliff over an abyss. But
when he stood on the other side, smiling, and reaching
out his hand toward her, then she closed her eyes and
jumped, without knowing why. During their engagement, when he was working on *The Abduction from the
Seraglio*, the opera whose main character bore her name
– that was pure coincidence and yet like an omen for her
– during their engagement he explained to her how he
transformed powerful feelings into music. That was on
the sofa in "The Eye of God." He jumped up and ran
around the room, flailing with his hands, as always. It
looked as if he were trying to catch flies, and his hair got
all messed up. Then he sat down at the piano and played
her an aria, Osmin's aria, and he imitated a bass with his
light voice, and they both laughed. Then he grabbed her
and kissed her. Sophie came in and stood there dumb-

founded.

What he explained to her then he had also written to his father. She should read it again – but not now. She did not want to stand up anymore now, her feet were hurting.

She put the letters back in the envelope. One page would not go in, and she pulled it out again. Why did it not fit. They were all in there before. How clumsy she had become. That was probably because she had to use one of her hands to support herself.

"What are you looking for?"

She turned around, lost her balance, caught herself on the edge of the desk just in time. She was all red in the face, Sophie asserted. Should she call a doctor so he could bleed her? One cannot be too careful, an attack of suffocation like that....

Don't be silly, she wanted to say. But she stopped herself and mumbled instead, "Give me a hand. Something got caught."

"Were you reading those old letters again? That gets you too riled up. You remember the last time...." Sophie picked up the page and read in an undertone, "Just picture to yourself that rascal...."

"I told you to help me put them away, not read them."

"You're in a bad mood again today."

"I am not."

Sophie sighed.

If there was one thing Constanze could not stand it was that meek, pious sighing.

Sophie turned the letter over with a gesture much larger than necessary, as if to demonstrate that she would by no means read any further. The page fit into the envelope as if it were the simplest thing in the world.

"Actually, I wanted to go to the cemetery today," said Constanze.

"Are you sure that you feel well enough? It's chilly outside."

"It'll be a long time before it gets any warmer. Half a year."

"Indeed."

Simultaneously they started to laugh. Even at her age, Sophie still had that contageous chortling laugh. She went to the window, opened it, and stuck out her hand.

The air smelled good from the rain.

Constanze held on to the railing. Going down stairs had become a test of courage already years ago. But she tried to step firmly, not with those shaky old-woman's movements that she detested. Sophie went down a step ahead of her, turning around anxiously each time, just like a mother hen. Her neck, too, looked like an old hen's. Soon she would start to flap her wings.

They stepped out of the house, the cobblestones still glistening from the rain. A little boy slapped a stick into a puddle. Water splashed up and sparkled. He struck more vigorously, with a serious, watchful face. His pants and socks were dark with water. A cat strolled across the square, shaking its paws after each step.

Juden Street was crowded with people. Again and again people took off their hats and nodded respectfully.

"It's really annoying when you have to greet someone every two steps." Constanze nodded affably. Sophie smiled her smallest smile.

It would be a lot more annoying not to have anyone's greetings to acknowledge.

The sun was not warm. But it did gild the city, making windows light up, the thick drops on a lantern, the crown of a Madonna above a house door. The gates to the vaults were standing open. Constanze said that she had to pick up something at Hagenauer's Variety Shop.[23]

"Luise can pick it up tomorrow so you don't have to go out of your way. You only torture yourself by walking."

Constanze placed her walking stick somewhat more emphatically on the pavement. "I know what I'm doing."

They walked the short distance to Getreide Street. How narrow it was here. Not to be compared with the beautiful open square in front of her building. The windows of the apartment on the third floor were open. Too bad that the Novellos[24] had not moved in there. Decent people, and the days with them had been so nice. They had come from England on a pilgrimage to Mozart. That is what they said themselves. With what respect Novello took each thing that she showed him in his hands – the letters, the pictures, the ink well. Like holy relics. He almost fell down on his knees. And he was an important man in London, respected as a musician and publisher, and wealthy too. How well he knew Mozart's music. He knew what key each piece was written in, he hummed the themes as if he had composed them himself. He was interested in everything, he wanted to know everything. Yet he did not ask any unwelcome questions. He was very discreet and full of respect for her. When she gave him a lock of Mozart's hair, he stood there and his eyes filled with tears. It was a long time before he could express his gratitude. Then he took a gold pin out of his necktie and requested the honor of presenting it to her.

His wife could have become a friend, although she was so much younger. A friend or a daughter. The warmth with which she approached Constanze, embraced her and cried. Constanze herself had to cry. It was a odd feeling, holding a stranger in your arms and crying. An English woman to boot.

How long ago was that? Certainly more than ten years. It was in the same year that Nannerl[25] died.

"Don't you feel good?"

"How so?"

"You're not walking."

"Why shouldn't I feel good? But something just occurred to me. Do you remember the Novellos?"

"Of course, the conductor from London and his wife. They were here at the same time as Wowi. So elegant, both of them. One really couldn't tell that she had had eleven children." Sophie chatted on, remembering in all detail a green dress that Mary Novello had worn, the wonderful lace around the neckline, the exquisite Turkish shawl. Sophie would have liked to have one like that herself, but it was in no way affordable.

They walked slowly up Linzer Street, the incline was slight, yet noticeable. They had time. It was pleasant to stroll along, the motion drove the cold out of one's bones.

It was at least ten years ago since the Novellos had been there. 1829, twelve years ago.

Vincent Novello's pin had been reworked into a pendant for her necklace. He was so happy when she told him about the plan; he said, it was a special honor for him. His wife looked at him lovingly and pressed Constanze's hand.

"You know," Sophie said, "I asked myself more than once whether he wasn't in love with you."

"Are you crazy? The man is twenty years younger than me."

"So what?" The corners of Sophie's mouth turned up. "You know – love strikes as it will, and all that. Think of Carl."

No, she did not want to think of him now. Not about him and his unfortunate love of a much older woman. Unfortunate? Oh yes, unfortunate, precisely because it was requited. Without that woman, Carl would perhaps have come to Vienna, would have made a career. Would he have?

And who sent him to Livorno, Constanze asked herself. You yourself sent him there. You see.

Sophie changed the subject, apparently noticing that she had said the wrong thing. It was almost uncanny how often she could read Constanze's thoughts; or at least she knew when she was treading on dangerous ground. Sophie avoided any and all confrontation, not so much because she was compliant – although she was that, too – but because almost nothing in the world seemed important enough to her to risk the danger of ill feelings.

"I still believe that he was in love with you, at least a little bit. The way he always took your arm; even at that time when we walked along this street, do you remember? Although you were still very spry, God knows. I always lagged along behind like a little puppy with its tongue hanging out, and I had a hard time keeping up with you."

Yes, she had been light on her feet, had loved to dance. The first Mardi Gras with Mozart.... He made such a good harlequin. It had been especially nice at Baroness Waldstätten's.[26] There she did not have to be so careful about every word; there she knew she was accepted. They had danced all night long there on more than one occasion. Mozart was in such a good mood. He actually made pantomines out of the minuets, the contredanses, the polkas, and the regional dances. She went along with it, self-consciously at first, but then with increasingly greater enthusiasm, until at some point, heated and excited, they fell into each other's arms in a corner.

"He acted as if one couldn't let you take a single step alone," said Sophie.

"He? Who?"

"Good grief, whom are we talking about then? Novello, of course. Are you sure we shouldn't turn around?"

"Of course, I'm sure. Stop asking me, or I'll get

mad."

"All right, all right. Do you remember the last evening before they left? When we met them in a restaurant, together with Mona.[27] You had given him an aria...."

Constanze nodded. "It was *Al desio*, with a cadenza that Mozart had written for me, a copy in his own hand. Afterwards I almost regretted having given it away, since later there was almost nothing left of the mountain of manuscripts. But at the moment, you know, I simply had to give it to him. Then I wondered whether I should have done that, whether I shouldn't have saved it for Wowi. But what's the use, done is done."

"They will preserve and honor the score. Wowi doesn't have any children anyway, and who knows what might have become of it."

That was probably supposed to be some sort of consolation. It was not, though.

They reached the Sebastian Cemetery and sat down to rest on a ledge of the wall in the evening sun. Constanze closed her eyes.

She saw herself with Sophie and Mona going into the "Ship"[28] where the Novellos had stayed. It was one of those mild summer evenings, when the fragrance of even far-away roses penetrates the narrow streets. As they entered the restaurant, Vincent Novello had jumped up, his napkin falling to the floor. He came toward Constanze with long steps, took her hand and kissed it respectfully. The waitress brought the meal. Novello apologized profusely, and his wife asked whether the ladies would not show them the honor of dining with

them. Never before had Constanze felt so strongly that
her mere presence could be something of value. As if she
were a princess, at the very least a princess. That was
what she thought at the time and ever after when she
recalled the visit.

They sat and chatted like old friends, in French. It
went surprisingly well, except sometimes Constanze
could not remember the right words. Novello ordered a
bottle of wine, and they drank to a future happy reunion.
Mary Novello pressed her hand and promised to learn
German by the next time. She would so much like to ask
about things, she said, that one could answer only in
one's native language. Vincent described his house in
London to her and implored her to regard it as her own
when she, as he hoped, came to visit; perhaps together
with Wowi, who would certainly find influential friends
in London, and whom he had come to regard as an
exceptionally fine young man. They discovered that they
were able to laugh about the same things. Suddenly they
saw how late it had become. She realized that it was
difficult for her to say good-bye. Two weeks ago she did
not even know these people, and now they were so
close. Ever since Nissen's death she had not felt so
relaxed in the company of others. But it was time to go.

Novello insisted upon accompanying her. She said
all the right things – that it was not necessary, that there
were three of them, and that he had to be on his way
early in the morning. She said all of that with conviction;
it was true too, and she did not want him to go to any
trouble. Besides, the night was clear, and the moon was

shining.

He bowed in front of her. It was not every evening, he said, that he had the opportunity of enjoying the company of someone who had shared a life with Mozart.

Then she took his arm. He would write of it later, "*so warmly ... as if I were her own brother.*" She stumbled several times while walking, but as she turned around to look, there was nothing there on which to stumble. Novello said that now she would have to admit how good it was to have an arm to lean on. Of course, it was good to have someone to lean on for support. She had missed that for a long time. Ever since Nissen's death. He too had offered her support from the very beginning, had brought order into her chaotic financial records, had helped her with correspondence. It was so hard to strike the right tone in letters to publishers. They all thought they could take advantage of a widow. He had also corrected her spelling, which was more than necessary; the many mistakes were already then an embarrassment to her. Above all, however, Nissen had assumed responsibility for the boys, had even helped Wowi with his schoolwork. That was necessary too, since although he was not dumb, he was lazy. Nissen himself did not have any children, although he would have made a good father.

Nonsense. He was a good father, for Mozart's and her sons. And both of them recognized that, Carl as well as Wowi. Recognized it with gratitude.

"George Nicholas von Nissen, Royal Danish State Councilor, Knight of the Dannebrogk Order," she had

had chiseled on his gravestone. And underneath that, "Husband of Mozart's Widow."

"As it stands," said Sophie, "the State Councilor is less important."

Constanze shook her head involuntarily. There she was again, Sophie's uncanny gift of pinpointing precisely the thing that was half-consciously going though her own mind.

But it was true. It really was true. To be the husband of Mozart's widow, that was the most important thing in Nissen's life. His life work was writing a biography of Mozart. He had worked on it up until the very end, increasingly faster, increasingly more determined. As if he knew that time was running out. He wrote to everyone under the sun. Every detail was important to him. As patient as he was otherwise, he became increasingly impatient if she could not answer one of his questions to his satisfaction.

It had been so much work simply to sort through the piles of paper. Papers were lying around everywhere and only got more mixed up with each move.

"Husband of Mozart's Widow."

When she ordered the inscription she was so confused that she even made a mistake with Nissen's birthplace. Hardensleben instead of Hadersleben. But husband of Mozart's widow, that was important. Much more appropriate than husband of Constanze, neé Weber, widowed Mozart.

Was she Constanze for him? Yes, that too. But first of all the widow of the man whom he worshipped. The affection that he showed her was actually always directed toward him too, the dead man. He was the one Nissen was looking for, even in her arms.

Not that she was complaining.

She could not have wished for a better husband. Not at all.

How concerned he was about her reputation. He crossed out passages in Mozart's letters that seemed to him too intimate. At the same time he insisted that posterity had a right to know everything about Mozart. Everything? Sometimes she was sorry about the crossed-out passages, but not because of posterity; that did not concern her. She could not imagine a time after herself any more than she could a world before her time. She was sorry about the deletions for her own sake. Precisely in those passages one could sense something of Mozart, of his laughter, his cheerfulness, his fun, of the one whom she knew. But the one who wrote the music that was said to be immortal by an increasingly large number of experts – that person she knew much less well. When she read what some people wrote about him, she herself could not believe that she had held him in her arms.

In December it would be fifty years since he died. He was far away, but no longer so completely distant as shortly after his death. Strange. All those who spoke and wrote about him made him only more of a mystery to her, until she could hardly even think of him anymore and was surprised to be called by his name. Nissen had brought him closer to her with his insistent questions, even if they seemed at first to cover over the last traces of memory. His questions were insistent and cautious at the same time, and they ceased only with his death. As disconcerting as they had been to her at the time, those eternal questions, she came to miss them. She began also to sense that the answers were as important to her as they were to Nissen.

That was the time when she began to dream about Mozart. He was never directly present, but had just gone out of the room. The feather in the inkwell still shook because he banged the door so stormily behind him. Or he was expected back any minute.

"For his fiftieth anniversary I'll have a festive requiem mass read in the cathedral," said Constanze. "Best of all would be if Wowi would direct the *Requiem* again."

Sophie nodded. "I get cold chills just thinking about the *Requiem*."

"Of course we know now that it was only the servant of Graf Walsegg."[29]

Of course she knew that Graf Walsegg commissioned the *Requiem* and wanted to claim it as his own, said Sophie; but that did not explain anything. Constanze herself had told how it sent shivers down her spine as she saw the gray man standing there before their departure for Prague. Maybe it was in fact the servant, or someone else who looked like him. How was a person supposed to ascertain that?

Sophie clutched her shawl more tightly around her. Finally, she herself had experienced something that did not admit of explanation. She had written it to

Constanze, as well as to her dear, now deceased, husband, the best brother-in-law in the world to her sister.

Constanze nodded; she remembered exactly, she said. But Sophie would not let herself be held back. All morning long, she said, she had had to think about that day. Everything appeared before her mind's eye; as clearly as, no, much more clearly than if she were walking right now on Rauhenstein Street. She could see every stone on the ground, even the cat that disappeared behind the corner of the house when she came; and the baker's boy with his bread basket on his back, and the worn-out place on the fifth step.

"It was the fourth."

No, the fifth. She knew that exactly because she had slipped and had had to catch herself on the railing. Then she had turned around and thought, that could have been a bad fall, down five steps of stone.

Constanze did not contradict her, and that led Sophie to cast an anxious glance sideways. "Are you cold? Do you want to go home?"

No, she did not want to go home. The slanted rays of sunshine drew clear lines in the grass. A flock of birds flew over the cemetery. She had no idea what kind of birds they were. She would have liked to know now, although she had never been interested in such things before. Sophie talked and talked. How she had come running, completely out of breath. And then she stood in front of the house door and did not dare to knock for fear of what she would find. After the episode with the lamp she did not have any hope anymore. But Constanze must understand why she had waited so many years before she told her about it. She was afraid to irritate her sister even more. Constanze at the time was out of her mind as she threw herself over the corpse. Baby Wowi was crying in his crib, but she was deaf, blind and deaf.

The 4th and the 5th of December 1791 were obliterated from her memory, also the days immediately thereafter. She was dependent upon the reports of others, above all on Sophie's. But it could not be right, it must have been different, at least in some details. Sophie maintained with the same certainty as with everything else that on the morning after Mozart's death throngs of people came by, crying and mourning for Mozart. Constanze knew from reliable sources that that was not true. She even believed to remember that it was a part of her despairing agony that there were so few with whom to share it.

She had felt indifferent toward that last day for a long time. Nothing would bring Mozart back. There were a few vague memories: the closing commissioner who went through the rooms and took inventory; how he picked up a glass candle and set it down so precariously close to the edge of the table; how he feelingly handled Mozart's white linen coat. Pale faces, cold hands that shook hers. No memories at all of the children; someone must have taken care of them. Today, for sure, she wanted to have her own memories, but there were none in the offing. Other things, long forgotten, came back, but that week remained blotted out.

"Snuffed out," said Sophie. "The lamp was snuffed

out, as if it had never burned. No spark remained in the
wick." That was how she had described it in the longest
letter of her life, twenty years ago when Nissen asked her
for details about the day. If one wrote something down,
was it then fixed for all eternity, a memory that could not
be corrected anymore? Did it become petrified? Was it
necessarily so because she had written it like that?
Regardless of how it really had been?

"There was definitely no draft in the kitchen, I swear
to it," said Sophie. She had just sat there staring into the
flame and thinking that she would like to know what
Mozart was doing. And as she was thinking and looking
into the light, it went out. As truly as she was here now.

Constanze nodded.

Maybe she should never have gone to Baden. But
he had insisted on it, purely out of concern for her health.
At the time she had been weakened by Wowi's birth.
And now she was going on her eighties! It was like a
bad joke; as if heaven wanted to prove those people right
who had always said that she was not really sick, she just
wanted to have a good time in Baden.

"When I walked into his room, he called to me immediately: '*Ah, dear Sophie, how glad I am that you
have come. You must stay here to-night and see me
die!*'"

Sophie crossed her arms in front of her chest and
looked up at the gold-bordered clouds, as if she were
reading from them. "I tried to be strong and to talk him
out of it, but he had an answer for everything: '*Why, I am
already tasting death. And, if you do not stay, who will

support my dearest Constanze when I am gone?"'

Did she mean to sound so self-satisfied, or was that only imagination? When her sister spoke about Mozart's death, Constanze always had the feeling that she generously shared something that rightfully belonged only to her. But Sophie had in fact stayed by her, and when Sophie's husband died on the same day as Nissen, she came as quickly as she could from Slovenia to Salzburg. She was a good sister, the best. If only she would be quiet.

"In my will I have bequeathed you the big hanging clock that goes for a week at a time," said Constanze. "Later the boys will get it."

Sophie apparently was not yet finished. She vacillated between feeling irritated by the interruption and grateful for it. Her face showed plainly what she thought and felt. In all of her seventy-four years she had not learned to dissemble.

"And you get my clothes and my linens too, and everything in the kitchen. You have a copy of the will. I'm sure that Carl and Wowi will carry out my wishes faithfully, but still it's good to have it down on paper."

"Oh, Constanze, whoever said that you won't outlive me? I become very frightened when you talk like that."

Sophie took Constanze's hand, but she did not thank her.

"You're the younger one. Five years younger. And besides, you didn't go through all those pregnancies and births."

Constanze turned to face Sophie.

A shadow came over her sister's face, her eyes became veiled. It was her great sorrow that she did not have any children. She did not know that children are no defense against loneliness.

Sophie sighed.

Constanze stretched out her arthritic fingers as much as possible. Her thumb and forefinger would neither stretch nor close entirely. She looked at her hands, in which the blue veins became increasingly protruding. There was a new dark spot.

Mozart had had nice hands. As delicate as a woman's. One could not tell by looking at them how strong his grip was, especially in the bass register.

"Should we go home?," Sophie asked. "I'm afraid you'll get cold."

"Whenever you get cold, you always push it off on me. Who knows how often we'll still be able to sit outside."

Sophie bent her head down.

Constanze poked around with her cane in the gravel.

It had been an awfully long time since Wowi had written. He seemed so depressed during his last visit. When he thought no one was looking, the corners of his mouth turned down, his narrow pretty face looked troubled and was already beginning to get lax in its contours. His movements seemed tired too. As if he knew in advance that nothing he did would lead anywhere, that he would run and run but never arrive. There was no excitement in him, no looking forward to the next day. Sometimes it seemed to her as if he were much older than she. It had begun so promisingly, the little son of a big man who mesmerized the people with his charms. "People expect too much of me," he said. "My name has become a burden." The name that was supposed to open all doors for him.

He had not said anything more about Juszinka during his last visit, and she did not ask. Strange that both sons should fall in love with older, married women. How long had it been now since Carl's daughter died? Constanze had held her granddaughter only once. That was when she visited Carl in Milan, the Royal and Imperial Prefect, a stranger. She was touched by the fact that he had given his daughter her name. Maybe she should not have sent him on the business apprenticeship. Wowi maintained that between the two of them, Carl was the better pianist.

It would be nice to see grandchildren grow up. She had had so little of her own sons. When van Swieten[30] took Carl to Prague, shortly after Mozart's death, she was glad to know that he was cared for, glad that other people made decisions for her. Van Swieten certainly knew what was right. If not he, then who? Five years later Wowi too went to Prague, to the Duscheks.

Josefa Duschek[31] had been the object of her envy, completely different from the soubrettes and chambermaids with whom Mozart had otherwise played around – and more than that. Josefa Duschek, the beautiful, confident, successful woman, for whom he had written

"Bella mia fiamma" and "Ah, lo previdi." Most other women paled in comparison to Josefa Duschek. She was also supported by a general wave of popularity and stood at the center of every social event.

Actually, I should be grateful to her, thought Constanze. She did a lot for us, for Mozart and the boys. She was always hospitable toward me too.

When a woman stands at the center of a stage, even if that stage is only a living room, then she is beautiful, regardless how she actually looks. Even the Cavalieri,[32] the one-eyed woman who was ugly and widely recognized as such; even she could make people believe that two men were fighting over her when she stood on stage in the role of Konstanze. Strange.

Recognition and applause were powerful beauty treatments, much more effective than all the lotions and dyes and make-up. Not only for women. When Mozart celebrated the triumph of his *Figaro* in Prague, he had gotten bigger, someone to whom you reached out your hand rather than tapping him on the shoulder.

"I didn't bring flowers to Nissen's grave today," said Constanze.

There she was sitting by Nissen's tombstone and thinking about Mozart. But Nicholas would probably not have minded that. Certainly not. How often had he pressed her to recall a particular occasion, something that Mozart had said or she said to him. And when was that? Nissen asked again and again, and she did not know the answer. The days and the years ran together. It was seldom that a particular event surfaced in the broth.

When so, then it was usually nothing that could be told, nothing that one could nail down with words. At the time when I wore my blue dress. Then when I was pregnant. With six births in eight years, that was no precise method of dating. Pregnant with which child? I don't know.

Now and then islands would emerge, clearly lighted like stages. She and Mozart were acting on them, sometimes other people too. But she did not always know in which piece they were playing.

She knew that she, dissolved in tears, had severely reproached him; she still felt the irritation in her throat. Reproaches because of a woman? Because of his family? He did not try to defend himself, he just let her talk. That angered her even more, and she got herself tangled in empty accusations. At some point he would take her hand, kiss her eyes, kiss her cheeks and make silly little noises until they both had to laugh. But there were also serious quarrels.

There was the letter. Precisely that one, why had Nissen not destroyed it? He who was so careful that no shadow should fall on Constanze. Why had she not burned it herself, like a number of others? She did not know. She had read the letter so often that she saw it in front of her:

"You have no reason whatever to be unhappy. You have a husband who loves you and does all he possibly can for you. As for your foot, you must just be patient and it will surely get well again. I am glad indeed when you have some fun – of course I am – but I do wish that

you would not sometimes make yourself so cheap. In my opinion you are too free and easy with N.N.[33] ... and it was the same with N.N., when he was still at Baden. Now please remember that N.N. are not half so familiar with other women, whom they perhaps know more intimately, as they are with you. Why, N.N. who is usually a well-conducted fellow and particularly respectful to women, must have been misled by your behavior into writing the most disgusting and most impertinent sottises which he put into his letter.... Remember that you yourself once admitted to me that you were inclined to comply too easily. *You know the consequences of that. Remember too the promise you gave to me. Oh, God, do try, my love! Be merry and happy and charming to me. Do not torment yourself and me with unnecessary jealousy. Believe in my love, for surely you have proofs of it, and you will see how happy we shall be.... Tomorrow I shall kiss you most tenderly.*

Mozart"

Nissen had crossed out the names, and she did not know anymore to whom it referred. She really did not know. Would one of them have been Süssmayr?[34] Probably. And the other? She did not understand herself. Anyone who read the letter must think that she had been unfaithful precisely when he needed her, since he had his head full of worries and disappointments. Why could she not remember?

Maybe nobody would want to read the letters anyway. The biography had not sold nearly as well as she had hoped. There were still three hundred copies in storage here, and who knows how many at Breitkopf & Härtel's,[35] and at Mechetti's.[36] Schlichtegroll,[37] that scoundrel, that liar and slanderer, he had made big money with the necrology. Necrology! It was corpse looting, a dirty low-down trick. And a person like that was a Professor, Privy Councilor, and member of the Academy of Arts and Sciences. But there was no law against it; neither was there anyone to protect a person, especially if that person was a woman. Mozart would have had something to say to the fellow that he would not have easily forgotten. Even now she could explode with anger when she thought about the fact that she had even increased his profits by buying up six hundred copies of his botched book in order to destroy them; although she certainly could have used the money for other things at the time, God knows. Niemetschek,[38] the good soul, who had treated Wowi in such a fatherly fashion, had good judgment about Mozart and also about her. But the biographers in general were a plague. They only wanted to cash in on his fame, to cook their own soup, so to speak. Feuerstein[39] too, whom she had asked to continue Nissen's work. How many letters had she written him, how much postage spent. So much trouble, so much time, so much money, and all in vain. He did not even answer, the lout. The publishers too only wanted to collect, not pay. And after Nissen's death they apparently thought they would have an easy time of it with her. But they were in for a surprise. They apparently thought that she was still little Constanze, the naive young girl. Let them think that. She had learned her lesson. Now people called her greedy. Especially André[40] who cut a good deal when she sold him the original manuscripts. She should have asked much more for them. It was bad enough that they played *Don Giovanni* from Augsburg to St. Petersburg, from Bratislava to Buenos Aires, from Neustrelitz and Weimar to Stralsund and Reval, without her getting a single cent for it. Not only that. In the last years of Mozart's life his operas were already being played all over Europe – and he had to write letters begging for money.

But she was no longer without means. Thank God. And if it was indelicate to look after one's interest and maintain a privilege, then so be it. She stuck out her lower lip, smiled inwardly to herself. By birth a Weber, daughter of Fridolin Weber,[41] who earned two hundred gulden as bass singer, copyist and prompter. Having to support his wife and five children on that, he could not afford to be delicate. She knew only too well what it meant not to have any money, to be afraid when there was a knock at the door. It might be a creditor, or the landlord coming to collect the rent. She knew too well how bitter poverty tasted, how nastily a quarrel could escalate, even if only over a pittance. She knew how awful it was to be sent to the store as a child without money, to have to take the side-swiping remarks in hopes that if the coffee or the sugar were already packed in the bag one would get to keep it. Nowadays, of course, she was quite well off. But that did not mean that she should be careless. Just as before, she should watch that no one took advantage of her and that she got what was coming to her.

Finally, she had to think of her sons too. They would someday be able to use every last cent. Was it wrong that she had no confidence in them? As great as her hopes for Wowi had been, it was clear that nothing would become of him. She wanted to cross herself, but then Sophie would have asked what she was doing. She let it go and did it only in her thoughts. Not that he was not talented, not at all. He was talented. Even Salieri, the old adversary, affirmed that, and dear Papa Haydn[42] said so too. What was missing was the will power, the drive, the belief in himself. If he had to give music lessons all day long, he complained, then all his ideas were destroyed, and not much remained. He needed peace and free time for composing, he said. When she recalled under what conditions Mozart had written his works....

The sons would remain sons, even if they lived to be a hundred years old. Always only sons, even when father and mother were long gone. And the worst thing was that they knew it.

It could be that Constanze did not think anything; that she just sat there and watched how the wind blew a leaf onto the grass, picked it up again and finally let it fall. That she automatically read the marble tablets on the stones: "Royal and Imperial Superintendent's Daughter," "District Court Judge's Son," "Royal and Imperial Chief Customhouse Inspector's Widow," and "Postal Service Manager's Wife."

Coldness arose from the ground. Constanze was

freezing.

"Let's go."

As always, they returned by way of the arcades and the church. They remained standing a moment in front of the gravestone of Theophrastus Bombastus von Hohenheim.

"We should have a Paracelsus as our doctor," said Sophie. "He would know what to do about your arthritis and my rheumatoid fever." She touched the brown marble, as if unintentionally, and let her hand rest on one of the scrolls. Constanze did not comment anymore on the fact that she could hardly channel any of the famous life power toward herself. Sophie touched the Paracelsus gravestone, Luise kissed the feet of St. Anthony, she herself held firmly to her rosary. Novello and his wife had kissed Mozart's portrait after they had carefully wiped their lips on their snow-white handkerchiefs.

They walked slowly down the street. The evening was surprisingly mild, and a young woman was selling flowers on the corner. The roses in her basket seemed to shine from within. A good-looking man carefully picked out a bouquet. "Do you think that the King of Bavaria will come for the unveiling of the statue?" Sophie asked, louder than usual.

Constanze thought it entirely possible, especially after the splendid reception that the King and Queen had held for her the previous year at the occasion of the gala performance of *Don Giovanni*.

"What will you wear?"

How was she supposed to know now what she

would wear? It had not even been established at what time of year the statue would be erected. "You should have a new dress made. Something especially nice." Sophie described in great detail a dark red dress that she had seen in a fashion print from Paris. It had beautifully embroidered sleeves and an enhancingly high collar, frilled; something like the dress that Constanze wore in her portrait, but then again different.

"Dark red? Are you crazy? For a double widow? Besides, it's not worth it anymore at my age."

It was really about something else. It was always really about something else. They remained standing on the bridge over the Salzach. They looked down into the water, following a current until it disappeared and then following another one. Branches and boughs hung on the pillars of the bridge, around them were tiny whirlpools.

Something moved in one of the nests of driftwood, fluttering and beating. It took a long time before the women realized that it was only a piece of cloth.

As they arrived at Michaelis Plaza, the church bells began to ring, causing the air to vibrate.

It was a deep satisfaction for Constanze each time when she reached the apartment building. How elegantly the staircase swung up to the upper story, commanding the space, not narrow and steep as in most buildings, but pleasant to ascend, even on tired old legs.

Sophie slipped into the kitchen. She was apparently convinced that her presence was necessary and Luise would be helpless without her. Luise, on the other hand, often complained that Sophie was always in the way, so it was her fault when the meal was not on the table on time. But Luise was not even there today. What was the reason this time? Some nameday or another.

Constanze sat down in her chair, nodded to the picture of Nissen. Poised and serious, he looked at her over his red uniform. The high collar was appropriate and becoming to him. He had maintained his composure in all of life's situations, even when Copenhagen was besieged and bombarded by a thousand canons. Sometimes he seemed to her to be a teacher, a strict but fair and loving teacher. She had much to thank him for. From him and from others while by his side she had gained respect, felt herself taken seriously. He was a person whom others asked for advice, whose advice they also accepted, a person for whom servants opened doors before they were asked, a person to whom hotel keepers gave the best room, for whom they put on a clean tablecloth. She enjoyed all of that, above all, however, his loving care. He understood how much she looked forward to any message from Carl, and he had implored her son to send her a gift for their wedding. It was only by chance that she found out about that. Dear good Nicholas. His embraces too were serious and cautious. Never in her experience did he let himself go, nor did he ever lose his composure.

You could have used a man like that, Constanze said to the portrait of her sister-in-law. Then maybe you would not have become so bitter. How you sit there with your fancy hair-do. You don't look very happy; rather a bit stilted around the mouth, you know-it-all. Or disappointed? You certainly had reason to be, Anna Maria Mozart. Always the perfect daughter; that was no fun, but you never resisted. You obediently did what was expected of you. You played when your father told you to, and when you started to improvise, it was regarded as too "bold." You were not allowed to marry the man you loved because he didn't have any money. The man you got was bad-tempered and strict, with five children from two previous marriages. The children didn't like you, and they made things difficult wherever they could. You also buried two children. Johanna was already six. You knew her, knew how she laughed and how she talked. You stood up for her against her half-brothers, had plans for her, and then ... nothing. I feel sorry for you when I think of you today. What did you have from life? Success at first, the shimmering concert halls with candles and crystal and golden mirrors. The ladies and gentlemen in silk who applauded you, admired you, even if not so much as your little brother. You, of course, were older, and at twelve a child is no longer picked up and kissed by Her Royal Majesty as he was. But from then on it was downhill, sometimes faster, sometimes more slowly. Finally, you lay in your bed, transparent, and could hardly lift your hand; blind and helpless in your bed. And the continual headaches, sickness to the point of vomiting, days in the darkened room, and only your strict father for company. He loved you, certainly he loved you, perhaps more than his son. But you were only the daughter, not the hope for his own fame. Even the most perfect daughter, and that you certainly were, is still only a daughter. I would like to have been your friend, Nannerl, because you were Mozart's sister; because I wanted to belong, finally to belong somewhere; not have to be ashamed, not have to do quiet penance for the disorder in the room, for the glassy look of my mother, for the shabbiness, the torn covers on the chairs, the spot on the tablecloth, the worn-through arms in father's suit coat, his humble attitude, the glasses with the chipped edges. I was always on the side, you were in the middle, without question. Thus I saw you and envied you. Thus I sewed you the bonnets and knitted you the bands and bought you a heart with an arrow. It was not worth much, but more than I could afford. I didn't have any idea of the rejections and disappointments you had, how your world flickered and shattered into headaches. I never had headaches, at least not that kind. I sensed only your disapproval, your coolness. It didn't occur to me to question where it came from. When I began to understand, it already was too late; you were petrified. Then my sympathy would have irritated you if you had known about it. You were too big for me, do you understand? You hurt me from the very beginning. Even the way you walked through a room made me feel small and unimportant. You were so strict, so unwavering in your judgments, so entirely without "ifs" or "buts." Or perhaps not? I know it made you happy when Wowi came to visit and held your hand which couldn't grasp anything anymore. You loved your brother. How did it happen then that you withdrew from him when he refused to obey his father? Because he married me? Did you have to choose between father and brother?

We were two old women in a small town; two old women, both alone, both still – or again, after all these years – circling around one man, whom you knew at the piano and I knew in bed. Excuse me, Nannerl, but that's how it was. That's how I knew him. That too was a part of him and not the least important part. Was that the reason you resented me? I did not drag him down with my sensuality. Mark my words. The sensuality belonged to him, just as his music belonged to him. He was no pure spirit. Do you think that a pure spirit could have written those operas? Do you really think that? Perhaps it was also because we did what you wanted to do but didn't dare; because we fought for our love and made our own way, whereas you were obedient. Oh I know, you could say that I was not worthy of his love, I wasn't good enough to love. Who is then good enough to love? Who even knows what love is, and what only confusion, youth, and infatuation?

I was not unfaithful to Mozart when I married Nissen. Not before that either when I lived with Nissen without the blessing of the Church. Should I have declined the pension? It was hard enough to get along on the money we had, and without Nissen's prudence it would not have been possible at all. But you don't have any idea of that. How could you? No, I was not unfaithful to Mozart with Nissen. On the contrary. Even if I had wanted to, I could not have forgotten him for an instant, day or night.

If we had gotten to know each other better, I could

perhaps have explained it to you. Especially to you. But it's hard to understand something fully if one always has to think with one's mouth closed. Some things have to be said out loud in order for a person to think them. It has become clear to me in the meantime only because I can say it to you now, today, when you have been lying in St. Peter's Cemetery for twelve years. You didn't want to be buried in the family grave. But it would not have bothered me.

Constanze stood up. After reaching into the drawer she found what she wanted, and she hobbled back to her chair. Suddenly the pain in her foot became worse.

Listen to this, Maria Anna: *"Wolfgang was small, thin, pale in color and entirely void of all pretensions in body and build. Apart from music, he was a child, and he remained a child all his life. That was his main character trait on the negative side. He always needed a father, a mother, or someone to take care of him. He couldn't manage money. He married a girl who was unsuitable for him, against the wishes of his father. That was the reason for all the domestic disorder at the time of his death and thereafter."*

Do you remember? You wrote that yourself. And should I tell you something, Maria Anna Baroness von Berchtold zu Sonnenburg? I may have been unsuitable for him, and maybe I never understood him; but you didn't understand him either! He was not a child, and he would not tolerate a caretaker. I know that even if I don't know anything else. Perhaps he had never been a child. How can one be a child while traveling in coaches, in the salons, always on the road, always in the public eye, never really at home? Tell me that! You probably wanted to keep him a child, his whole life long. But he didn't go along with that. And should I tell you something else? The domestic disorder, that bothered him much less than the pursed lips and sidelong glances. He contributed his share to the disorder too, it wasn't only my doing. He knew orderliness only in his music. And when he finished writing it down, the pages literally flew.

Oh, Nannerl. On the anniversary of your death I'll place flowers on your grave and light a candle for you, if our dear Lord lets me live that long. It's only four weeks away.

Lord God, be merciful to her poor soul. Hail Mary. "When you go shopping tomorrow, Sophie, arrange for a mass at St. Peter's for Nannerl." Sophie nodded. She had brought in a tray with two bowls of soup and asked, as she did every evening, whether Constanze was satisfied with that. She received the usual answer: "At our age one doesn't need so much."

"I don't know," murmured Sophie. "I make the soup exactly according to the recipe of our dear departed mother, but it doesn't turn out so well as it did for her or for Josefa."[43]

Constanze blew on her spoonful of soup and said, even before tasting it, "It's very good."

They ate the soup in silence. Dusk settled in the room.

The chiming of the clock on the wall startled them

both.

"It's strange," said Sophie. "After all these years I still want to save the breast bones for Forti. Then I take them downstairs for the caretaker's dog who always looks so hungry. Do you remember Forti?"

"Of course. He barked a lot. But he was a good little fellow."

"And so clever. He always danced with excitement when I got ready to go outside. If I picked up the prayer book, however, he would crawl into the corner between the wardrobe and the door and sit there with his face to the wall, without even looking at me."

"Maybe he was a freethinker."

Sophie decidedly rejected that suggestion.

Both women had always lived with house pets. A house without a dog seemed empty to them. Both missed the welcome dances and the joyful barking when they returned home, missed the head on their knee and the expectant eyes. They had never discussed it with each other, but had silently and independently come to the same conclusion, that they were too old to get another dog. What would happen to him when I'm not here anymore, each thought to herself. And they would walk quietly on by if they happened to see young dogs playing. If dogs have a life expectancy of twelve years, then they themselves would be eighty-six and ninety-one. No, a dog was out of the question. Too late.

A year ago Sophie had brought home a canary, but it flew away, in the first week. Both of them, each for herself, tried to resist interpreting that as a bad sign.

"Sometimes when I wake up I still reach out my hand from the bed to pet him," said Sophie. "I think that Forti was the best dog among all those that I had."

Constanze nodded and in the midst of nodding asked abruptly, "Why don't you light a lamp?"

She saw too much in the shadows. All those who were not there anymore pressed in, and also those who had never been in this place; no ghosts, but memories that made the shadows too dense.

Sophie replied as expected, "With these newfangled matches it's no problem." Constanze could not remember her sister ever taking a match in hand without commenting on what a time-saver it was. "The servant girls today don't have any idea of what housework is. Nowadays any child can light a fire."

"How about a glass of punch?"

"That would be good since it's cold in here."

That was another topic they did not talk about. With every glass of wine, with every cup of punch, each of them worried that the other would think: Now she's starting that too. Just like our mother.

Sophie made good punch. One had to give her credit for that. Constanze held the glass with both hands and breathed in the aroma.

Mozart had drunk punch during the night when he composed the overture to *Don Giovanni*. Or was it *Figaro*?

Sometimes everything got mixed up and ran together. And the people who came and asked questions would say then: But you told it differently to someone else. That was on a different day too. Memories do not remain fixed. Sometimes a piece is added, sometimes a piece falls away. Some things suddenly become clear, so clear as if the sun were shining all too glaringly on parts of the past.

How old she had become. Older than her mother, older than her father, older than Leopold Mozart, older than Nissen, older even than Papa Haydn. Ancient.

But something was not right, could not be right. Yesterday was much farther away than the fourth of August fifty-nine years ago. That was the day on which she was married to Conductor Wolfgang Mozart (marital status: single) in St. Stephen's Cathedral in Vienna. She still felt the tears in her eyes and on her cheeks. May I blow my nose now, or not; that would make too much noise. And then the tears in his eyes. Even the priest began to cry and, of course, her mother. A mother-of-the-bride who did not cry – Caecilia Weber[44] would not sink that low. Even the gatekeeper blinked away the tears. Then they rode to Baroness Waldstätten's place for a reception – and suddenly it was a celebration. My, how they danced! Mozart could not get enough. He danced more and more wildly, and he even danced with her mother. Her mother was not a bad dancer. And she apparently forgot that just shortly before she had threatened to call the police and have her daughter removed from the Baroness's house.

"Do you remember Baroness Waldstätten?" Constanze asked, since all of a sudden she noticed the increasing stillness in the room. Even the candle sparkled loudly in this threatening silence, and Sophie sat there with folded hands as if waiting for a verdict. Startled, she spread out her fingers and nodded vigorously.

"Oh, yes." She ran her fingers through her gray hair, which seemed to rise to meet her hands. She looked disheveled, with her hair standing on end. "Of course I remember her. She was a beautiful woman, and so friendly. She never made you feel that you weren't good enough for her."

"You spoke differently at the time."

Sophie got red in the face. She still blushed as easily as a young girl, and then one forgot her wrinkles, her sunken cheeks, and her limp heavy eyelids. "What was I supposed to do? It was hard enough anyway for our dear mother and the guardian when you ran away. Nothing but quarreling and crying all day long."

"I did not run away. I was living with the Baroness for a month to take care of her when she was ill."

"But still mainly to get away from home!" maintained Sophie.

"You have no idea how awful it was. You didn't have to deal with that, you were always the little darling. I was the one on whom she took out her anger, about Louise, about the whole world. Josefa never paid much attention to it, so mother didn't harass her so much. I bet there wasn't a single day when I didn't go to bed crying. And how she complained about dear old dad, even after his death. She called him a loser. That hurt me the most."

"I always defended you when she complained about you," asserted Sophie.

"I certainly didn't see anything of that."

"But it's true."

What she could excuse in her mother least of all, said Constanze, was how her mother showed her father every day that she despised him. "At first she pestered him until he gave up his good position as magistrate, a remunerative, respectable position. And then she pinned his ears back because he wasn't successful in Mannheim. Was it after all his fault? Everybody knows how much intrigue there is in the theater, how no one lets anyone get away with anything. But she spoke as if his not singing the lead role was intentional and only to aggravate her. She nagged and nagged, she put him down in front of others, and she said that he was equally as poor a singer as he was a father to his family. Then she demanded that he go to the Elector and insist on his rights. How could he possibly do that? Where was he supposed to get the courage?"

"He was lacking in self-confidence," said Sophie. Constanze believed to be hearing an echo of her mother's voice.

"And who robbed him of that self-confidence?" She asked more sharply than she had actually intended.

"You are so hard on our good mother. She doesn't deserve that, poor lady."

"I forgave her for everything she did to me. But our father, she has him on her conscience."

"Constanze!"

The soft-spoken friendly man with his self-conscious smile. He who lit up when he saw her. He who never lost his patience when she made a mistake while playing the piano. He who beamed when she sang a difficult passage correctly. He who always gave her the best things to eat. In Vienna he was never happy anymore. He wandered like a shadow through the house. He hardly talked anymore after the day he found out that the position promised him "according to his artistic abilities" was that of cashier at the theater. And mother said at the time, you know you only have Louise to thank for the position.

Before his death he gave Mozart his Molière books. That was after Aloysia had sent Mozart away, the small man with the black overlay of mourning on the gold buttons, who had returned from Paris disappointed. Constanze saw him standing there, clicking his right heel against his left, saw him go to the window and drum on the windowsill, ridiculous in his fidgety behavior, even smaller than usual. She saw him furiously playing the piano and heard him singing loudly: "Whoever doesn't like me can lick my arse!"

She saw herself cover her mouth with her hand, as if she herself had said something for which she at fourteen would have had her mouth washed out with soap. But she was truly horrified about Aloysia, who in February had talked about eternal love and faithfulness and who said later, laughing coldly: He could not do anything for her. Aloysia told him that she had an engagement as prima donna in Munich and earned twice as much as he.

"How brief eternities can be," said Constanze.

"What do you mean?"

"Oh, nothing. I was thinking about Louise."

Sophie nodded her head. "Grant them eternal rest, o Lord."

"And may perpetual light shine upon them," added Constanze.

How long would this eternity last?

How long did Louise's great love for Lange[45] last?

But in the end, the beautiful, celebrated Aloysia, who had gone from one success to another, was dependent on the monetary support of Constanze.

No, she was not gloating over the misfortune of others. She had wished all the best for her sister and had not begrudged her success. That goes without saying. The money in her will amounted to thirty-five gulden and twenty kreuzer when she died two years ago. Aloysia Weber, who signed her first contract for one thousand gulden, at a time when her father earned two hundred gulden in an entire year.

The ways of the Lord are inscrutable.

Mozart himself had written about Aloysia, saying that she was a false, malicious person and a coquette; and he was certainly never mean-spirited. He continued to compose for her, even after that letter. He loved her voice. "She sings from the heart," he said. How many hours he had worked with her at that time in Mannheim, before his trip to Paris, while Constanze sat in a corner and sewed or mended or just listened. Louise and Josefa had learned to play the piano and sing already before Mozart's visit; but for her, Constanze, there was nothing left. Her mother was never willing to invest money in her education. But her father would have paid for some training after she had learned everything that he himself could teach her. He, certainly.

The mother of the prima donna Aloysia Weber stretched out like a cat in the glory of Louise's fame. She had no time for the other daughters. When Joseph Lange fell in love with Louise, the marriage could not come soon enough for her mother; and later she did everything she could to prevent just that marriage. A strange woman, her mother, full of contradictions, and she stood in the way of her own wishes.

"I think she was happy only when she had reason to be unhappy."

"Who?"

"Whom are we talking about? Our dear departed mother, of course!"

"She wanted to be happy as much as anybody else. The question is, whether that is possible. Were you ever happy, really happy?"

"Of course," said Constanze quickly. Of course?

"When?"

"When, when ... often."

"Give me an example."

"What's the matter with you today? You're ... oh, I don't know how you are.... I mean, in Mannheim once there was a parade. I must have been very little for I couldn't see anything. Then our good father put me on his shoulders, and I was taller than anyone else, and I could look down on them and see everything. And then, when Mozart composed the fugue for me and had never written a fugue before, and...." She broke off. "Many times," she said after a while. "I can't even count them all."

Sophie shook her head gently. It was superfluous for her to add: Twice for five minutes – that's a lot for eighty years. "I don't mean that there is no happiness in the world, large and small, but true joy ... I don't even know what that is."

Then Constanze could say, "You're ungrateful."

It felt good to say that. Sophie understood how she meant it. She nodded her head, stared into the light and was silent.

"Your punch will get cold."

Sophie obediently took a drink.

Constanze smiled. "Little Sophie and the Big Joy. That would be a fairy tale. Somebody should write it, if it doesn't already exist."

Sophie laid her small, dry, wrinkled hand on Constanze's hand for a moment. "When I hear Mozart's music, there are places, in the piano concerto, for example, that make me happy when I hear them. But afterwards there remains a strong yearning, as if everything should be different."

"Which piano concerto do you mean?"

Sophie hummed the beginning of a melody. Constanze hummed along. "C Major," she said then. "Yes."

A moth beat against the windowpane.

"His music is full of such passages," said Constanze. "I always knew that. Only I didn't know how great it was. How should I have known? I understood so little of it. I would have liked to learn more as a young girl, but there was no opportunity. And later I was always busy with other things, especially with having babies. Now I'm sorry. He would have liked to explain it to me."

"Your big belly must have stood in the way of your playing the piano, I could imagine," said Sophie.

Constanze laughed. "Towards the end, of course. But otherwise the problem was more that sitting for any length of time was painful for me. Especially in my back, and also in my legs. I think I felt the babies more in my legs than anywhere else."

Sophie laughed. "Your legs weren't that fat, after all. By the way, have you noticed how thin Wowi's hair has become? He'll soon have a bald spot."

"Can you imagine Mozart with a bald spot? As an old man, walking slowly with a cane and holding the musical score at a distance?"

"No."

"I can't either."

"It would not have fit him," said Sophie.

"I would have liked to know him as an old man." What would he have been like? Quieter? Like Joseph Haydn? No, definitely not – different. But he would have been successful. Many concerts were coming in just before his death – from Hungary, Prague, and England. Too late. She did not want to think about it. Not about his death. Constanze was grateful when Sophie began to talk again.

"I just can't believe that Carl is already fifty-seven. It

seems to me just yesterday when there was a knock on our door at four o'clock in the morning. Our dear mother – I can see her now – sat up in bed and crossed herself. I hope there hasn't been an accident, she called. I had to go and open the door, but she stood right behind me. There was a messenger from Mozart who said, it's happening. Mother was so excited that she couldn't button her dress properly, always got the wrong button-hole. 'My poor Constanze,' she called out again and again. We ran through the streets, since there weren't any wagons at that time of night. It was just starting to get light."

"That was Raimund. Carl was fifty-seven on September 21st."

"Of course. That's who I mean."

Her mother at the birth of her children. Then she was a totally different person. She knew exactly what to do. She held Constanze's hand and rubbed her back. That felt good, especially with the first birth, when Constanze thought that one was supposed to feel the labor pains in her abdomen; she was not prepared for the fact that they cut through her back. Her mother was so calm, so completely there. She talked to the midwife and spoke reassuringly with Mozart. Her hand was cool on Constanze's forehead, cool and firm. It was good to see her in the big chair, sewing a shirt for the baby in the pauses between contractions. Her anxiety fell away in the presence of her mother.

"The mother I had while in childbirth – that's the one I would have liked to have always."

"You see," said Sophie. "And you were jealous of me."

"Not of you. But you had it better than I at home."

"I had my share of trouble too."

"You were always mother's favorite."

"Me? Aloysia was the one she was proud of. She would have liked us all to be like her."

"Proud, yes, but you were the one she loved. As much as she could love."

Sophie put the palms of her hands together. It almost looked as if she were folding her hands. "Honor thy father and thy mother; that thy days may be prolonged, and that it may go well with thee," she said. "Mozart didn't hold anything against her. He became fonder and fonder of her, and she of him too. I can see him now, how he would come running with a bag of coffee and sugar. 'Here, mother dear, now you can have a little coffee party.' Toward the end she loved him like her own son, and mourned for him as for a son. I almost think that she mourned more for him than for our brother."

"I'm not saying anything. I would just like to know how you would talk if someone treated you as she did me in 'The Eye of God.' As if I were the most reprehensible thing on God's great earth. And at the same time I had to listen to father Mozart calling me a wretch. For that I would still today like to...."

"Don't get excited, Constanze. It's over. They're all dead. Grant them eternal rest, o Lord."

"And may perpetual light shine upon them." Sophie folded her hands in her lap. "Would you like another glass of punch before it gets cold?" Sophie's gaze wandered again to the portrait of the two boys above the couch. "Do you know what I envy you for?"

"What?"

"They will still think about you long after you are gone."

"You too. You're their favorite aunt, you always were."

"But that's different. Something of you lives on in them."

"But for how long? They don't have any children."

"If not yet, they still can. They're not so old...."

Constanze interrupted her sister decisively. "No. And maybe – maybe it's better that way."

Sophie kneaded her hands. After a while she stood up and got her knitting.

"You'll ruin your eyes."

"There's not much left to ruin. Who knows whether what we can still see is worth seeing. I think my eyes hurt because of everything I have already seen."

"Yes," said Constanze, "it's a crazy time in which we live. Pretty soon you'll be able to take the train all over Europe. And when you arrive, then what? That certainly can't be good. Imagine if they had had a train fifty years ago. Then they probably would have brought the revolution here too, and there would have been war everywhere. You wouldn't be safe anywhere."

"You're not anyway."

A dog barked, another one joined in, windows were thrown open, and someone ran across the square.

Shortly thereafter heavy steps echoed on the pavement.

Sophie leaned out the window, came back disappointed. "Could that have been a burglar? Nothing more to see."

"It could also have been a lover whom the father discovered."

"Or the husband."

"You would think of that."

Sophie hummed a melody from *Don Giovanni*.

"Deh, vieni alla finestra ..."

"Don Giovanni was always spooky for me," said Constanze.

"I wouldn't have wanted to meet him either," Sophie stated emphatically.

"Because you yourself couldn't pass the fire-test?"

"Who can? You? I don't think that Mozart believed in fidelity forever. Zerlina and Susanne, not to mention Fiordiligi and Dorabella."

"But Konstanze and Elvira and Pamina are faithful."

"They are, to be sure."

"And you?" Constanze leaned forward. "Were you faithful to Haibl?"[46]

"Of course!"

Sophie sat up to her full height, her nostrils quivering. She seemed comical and at the same time dignified in her indignation. After a few minutes she exhaled noisily. "I wasn't so young anymore; I mean, I wasn't young at all when I married.... And out in Diakovár there wasn't much temptation. If there had been ... no, I think I would have been faithful then too. Definitely. And you?"

"Me? It's not true at all what people say," said Constanze.

"What do they say then? I haven't heard anything."

"Stupid gossip. I don't even want to talk about it."

She had enjoyed it when a man looked at her. She knew that she was not beautiful. She had never been beautiful, not even as a young girl. *"She is not ugly, but at the same time far from beautiful. Her whole beauty consists of two little black eyes and a pretty figure."* She would have liked to be beautiful. Who wouldn't?

Even in Mannheim, things had been neatly divided up. Josefa was the diligent one who did the cooking, the sensible one who maintained the peace. Louise was the beautiful, talented one; our Aloysia, with her wonderful voice, her silky hair, her tender little nose and graceful movements. Sophie was the little darling. And she – simply Constanze. Without any special beauty or wit, without any special talent. Nothing special about her at all. Not like Nancy Storace,[47] the blond English woman, the first Susanna, as beautiful as an angel, and she sang like one too, with her marvelous dark-toned mezzosoprano, with that smile in her voice. Mozart got home later and later while rehearsing *Figaro* with her. Constanze always waited at home with her swollen legs, with her bloated face, with the spots on her cheeks, with the thrusts in her belly. When he finally came home he had such a satisfied smile on his face that she could not believe it was only from the applause of the musicians, who, even during rehearsals, applauded after an aria and celebrated him as master. Then he would laugh and kiss her on the nose

and not take her seriously. She was convinced at the time
that Storace was his mistress, a beaming beloved who
sang his melodies as if she herself had invented them in
that instant; no, not invented, but discovered, discovered
them deep inside herself. And then she had to sing them
out because there was not room inside her for so much
beauty. Next to Nancy Storace, any other woman – even
a more intelligent, more beautiful, and more important
one than she – would pale by comparison. Even in all her
jealousy, Constanze could not think of Nancy as bad or
petty. Then too Mozart spoke about a trip to England,
about contracts and operas and good opportunities for
earning money; and all she could hear was Nancy. That
was serious, much more serious than the episode with
Josefa Duschek.

Again and again she had grilled Mozart: "Did you?
Or didn't you?" As if the English woman would be less
of a threat if Constanze knew about it. Neither flattery
nor defiance could bring him to a confession, although he
was otherwise relieved when he could confess to her
what had happened with some girl in a corner
somewhere. But this matter was different. She had
sensed that at the time; had, however, still tried to fit it
into the pattern of his peccadillos.

How foolish of her.

On the score of the scene and the aria that he had
written for Nancy Storace's concert recital stood, in his
handwriting: "For Mlle. Storace and me." How the
piano embraced and caressed the singing voice; how
question and answer engaged each other and melted to-

gether, whereby each stood alone and was yet interwoven in the other, as if each were greater in the inter-
weave than alone.

The question whether Mozart had shared a bed with
this woman was not only superfluous, it was ridiculous.
One should be ashamed of oneself. Actually, it was
worse if they had not made love. Unfulfilled desire does
not go away. It remains alive even after the pain has
stopped.

But how should she have known that at the time?
She was so young, could not really think a matter
through. When she was pregnant she could not think at
all. Thinking was blocked by anxiety. That stood at the
end of every thought, the anxiety of birth, the anxiety of
death. Hardly was a person pregnant before people
started telling about so-and-so, who died in childbirth,
and so-and-so, whose child was deformed. And then the
heavy breasts, hot and painful and big. Sometimes she
thought she should have nursed her babies. There were
women who did that, and not just servant girls or farm-
ers' wives. But Mozart did not want to hear of it.

No, thinking was not possible with so much fear in
her body. Where should she have learned how to think?
Thinking was not viewed favorably.

A few months ago she had seen a young woman sitting at a clearing in the woods, holding her child in her
arms and nursing it. No, nonsense. That was in Gastein
and thus must have been a few years ago. She could
picture it all too clearly: the tiny hands that kneaded the
breast. The young woman stood up and apologized; she

had not expected anyone to be passing by, and the baby had cried so. Constanze sat down on the stump of a tree, using her aching feet as an excuse to stay there a while. She looked secretly out of the corner of her eye over at the big dark nipples and the sucking little mouth, and she felt a twinge in her own breast. She was almost seventy years old at the time. Crazy.

Anna Selina Storace. Nancy. She too was dead, had been for years. Whether the two of them met in heaven?

"In my Father's house are many mansions." That was the topic of Father Dechant's sermon last Sunday.

She only hoped that Mozart and Nancy Storace had separate mansions in heaven.

Immediately she felt ashamed. First of all that was blasphemy; and second, out of place at her age. How could she stand in front of Saint Peter with such thoughts in her head? She should be happy if he would give her the last broom closet. Nonsense. That is not how it was. That is not how it would be. "Very different from what we can imagine," the Father Confessor had explained to her. "Very, very different. But don't be afraid. God cares for His own."

What if she were not one of His own?

She went to mass every Sunday. Only when she was sick, really sick and not just not feeling well, did she miss church. It had been that way for years. But when she sat in church she often found it difficult to concentrate. It would suddenly occur to her that she should write to Mechetti in Vienna; they still owed her money. Or her gaze fell on the straw hat of the woman in the second row in the front. She had wanted a hat just like that. She had written to Carl in Milan about it more than once, but he never sent it, not he. He was probably busy with other things and did not think about making his mother happy with a hat. Or the old conflict with Johann Nepomuk Hummel[48] flared up again. He had been Mozart's pupil, had sat at their table and slept in their house. He had promised a thousand times to repay them; but when he was finally in a position to do so, he did not lift his little finger. He did not even include her in his will. And then she was frightened and sought comfort in her rosary. "Hail Mary, full of grace."

She obeyed the commandments. Certainly. But how was it with "Thou shalt not covet thy neighbor's house, nor anything that is thy neighbor's"? She still coveted, even now. Although she knew that the last shirt has no pockets, as Sophie was fond of saying. Her last shirt had been lying in the drawer for a long time, neatly folded; each year it was taken out, washed and ironed. Yet there was this urge in her to possess, even things that she could not use anymore. Dear Lord, forgive me. And forgive us our trespasses, as we forgive those who trespass against us. No, not just that. I have so much trouble forgiving. I carry a grudge.

"Because she always wanted to get in ahead of me," murmured Constanze.

"Who?"

"The Storace woman." Actually she had not wanted to answer.

"But she's been dead for a long time," said Sophie.

That's it, thought Constanze. That is exactly it. And I could not even blame him. Until death do you part, as is written. It parted us. No, it did not part us. It brought us together. But that is not right either.

"The bad part about getting old," said Constanze, "is not the aching feet and the bad memory. After all, what is so important that a person must necessarily remember it? The bad part about growing old is that nothing is for sure anymore, that everything could have been entirely different. Earlier I used to know at least a few things for sure."

"You are, nevertheless, becoming increasingly ideosyncratic," stated Sophie. "Increasingly stubborn, as befits an old woman like you. And me," she added quickly.

Constanze wrinkled her forehead, then shrugged her shoulders. "Maybe the reason I get more stubborn is that I don't know anything for sure. Thus I have to insist that I'm right. – Is there any more punch?"

It looked as if Sophie would stick her head into the pitcher.

"There's a little left. Be careful, or we'll both start to sing soon."

"It's half cold anyway."

"The rum doesn't diminish because of that."

It had been a good idea to have Sophie come to Salzburg. Her presence in the room felt good. Her laughter drove off the shadows. Her questions helped to make one's own more bearable.

"You know, it irritates me that I can't look at the person I was, as a grandmother looks at her favorite grandchild. I constantly want to teach her and correct her. Sometimes I look at her as if I were her mother-in-law who had wanted a different kind of woman for her son. As if I were her rival. That's very unpleasant."

Sophie laid aside her knitting. "But you are all of that: the little girl, the young woman, the widow. That hasn't changed. Just a little while ago I thought anyone who sees your profile would recognize you immediately."

"Maybe, especially in the dark."

Sophie had not understood a thing. And, as so often when she did not understand, she would not change the subject. "You have, of course, grown older, but a person gets older every day."

Constanze yawned. "I think it's time to go to bed. I'm tired."

Even that did not stop Sophie. "What you say reminds me of a hall of mirrors. I don't know where it was anymore; but you could see yourself in a mirror, and behind that see yourself again, like before, only a little smaller; and behind that again and again, smaller and smaller, until you didn't recognize yourself anymore, only a tiny dot and very weird."

"Yes."

"But a person really shouldn't think like that," Sophie continued. "It's dangerous, for you don't know where you'll end up. Do you know what I do when I'm tempted?"

"Tempted to think?"

"Tempted to think like that!"

"What do you do?" That was an offer of peace, and Sophie accepted it immediately.

"I clean out a drawer and put in new paper lining. When everything is nicely in place again, then an inner order is restored as well."

"But when that doesn't help?"

Sophie thought a moment. "When I was small I used to hide under the wing of my guardian angel," she said. "It was nice and warm there, and dark."

I got stuck someplace, thought Constanze. There was an idea that I didn't think through. I'm always distracting myself, going from one thing to another. It's not even Sophie who distracts me. But when I don't know anymore what the question was, it always seems very important, as if everything depended on it.

"I'd like to get organized," she said. "But I never seem to make it. If I clean out one corner it seems to pile up in another. And in the last corner is chaos."

Sophie looked around in the room. "It's not so bad in here. Luise is not exactly the most orderly person, but if one stays by it.... You should tell me what you want, and I'll do it."

"I don't mean the apartment."

"Oh, I see." Sophie leaned back in her chair.

"What was I talking about?" asked Constanze.

"Putting things in order."

"No, before that."

"Before?" Sophie lengthened the final syllable. It was clear that for her there could be absolutely nothing before order.

"Ten thoughts before that."

"I can't read your thoughts."

"Sometimes you can."

Sophie smiled happily.

It was simply too late when Constanze first learned to think. One needs words for thinking, not just the everyday words that she had at her command.

"We were talking about marital fidelity," said Sophie.

"That's right. I think that when a woman knows she's beautiful, she doesn't need the attention of other men. Then one is enough for her, or even a look in the mirror. But when one doesn't like oneself, then it helps to have the attention of others. It makes things easier."

Sophie shook her head decisively. "I always started to stumble when someone was watching me walk. As if there were suddenly many stones in the path."

"Weren't you ever jealous of our sister Louise? Didn't you ever want to be like her? Look like her? Sing like her?"

Sophie wrinkled her forehead. "No. I always thought that when I was as old as she, then I would be like her too. But I never got to be as old as she, you know, since she always got older in the meantime. Then I stopped thinking about it. It didn't make sense anyway, do you think?"

"And you never did anything that didn't make sense?"

"Sometimes, but then it wasn't the right thing."

Sense. One of those big words that she could not

deal with, although she used it, of course, like everybody else. But what did it mean? What did make sense? Did her life make any sense? She had tried once to talk to her Father Confessor about it. "Our life lies in God's hand," he said. "He will take care of the meaning if we keep His commandments." He suggested that she turn to the Virgin Mary.

Brooding about things was probably a symptom of old age, like the weakened eyes, the loose skin, the lighter sleep, the thousand other changes that so softly and imperceptibly creep over one. If you tried to look at them directly, they disappeared into nothingness, less than a shadow; and yet they were dangerous lurking beasts. The day was not far off when she would not be able to read anymore even in the clearest daylight; when not only most people but all of them would speak unclearly; when the stairs, which got higher every day, would finally be insurmountable.

"I'm hungry all of a sudden," she said.

"Do you want to eat so late at night?"

"Yes. But you don't have to get up. I'll get it myself. Do you want something too?"

But of course Sophie got up. Soon she was rummaging around in the kitchen, and the noise sounded as if she were enjoying it. She came back with a tray, which she carried as if in a ceremonial procession. She had arranged cold cuts in a flower pattern on a serving plate, from light pink to dark red, with small strips of cheese in-between. She set the board with the bread on the table, also two apples, some grapes, and a big pitcher of apple cider.

"Do you remember how we used to smuggle apples and bread into bed in Mannheim and eat under the covers?" asked Sophie. Constanze wanted to say no, but then the memory came back. She saw herself and her little sister in their long nightgowns, smelled the slightly sour odor of the old blanket and the camomille fragrance from Sophie's hair, felt the scratching of the coarse linen sheet.

"Yes, and I had to hold your mouth shut because you couldn't stop laughing when mother came into the room." They both started to giggle, enjoying the late meal like something forbidden, as if their mother could walk in any minute and scold them.

"Tastes as if it were stolen," said Sophie gleefully with a full mouth. She had to cough and almost choked on a piece of apple, which led to further laughing spells. They both hugged themselves and rocked back and forth. Sophie stood up, hurried to the door with even smaller steps than usual. "Excuse me," she blurted out. "With all that laughing I have to...."

The Mozarts would have said that more directly, Constanze thought.

She was almost surprised that standing up was as difficult as ever. She had forgotten how old she was and how tired her bones had become. She went to the window, opened it and leaned out. Moonlight shone on the square. A light wind was blowing from the mountains, it smelled like leaves and moist earth.

She thought of the vineyards in Baden, the fog settling in, the golden light on the grapes, the dark pine woods. Once she picked a resinous drop from a big stem, rolled it between her fingers until the ends were black and sticky. It took days to get her fingers clean again. She recalled a chicory flower that had bloomed late, with blue stars between the dry grasses. A lazy, slow bumblebee. Carl's joy when a vintner gave him three big juicy grapes. The penetrating smell of piles of grapeskins, which went to your head. Or Süssmayr's teasing. The sulfur fumes in the baths. The self-discipline that it took to get in, and the wonderful lightness in all of your limbs when you were finally in. The pleasant sensation of warm water on your skin. The skin that she had now was not hers. It was much too big for her. Further, when she lifted an arm and smelled it, it had a strange smell. A dull odor, against which neither rose water nor lavender oil did any good.

A building door opened, a lantern lighted up the street and the niche next to the door. A young couple was standing there embracing. The ruckus started immediately. A man came out in a nightshirt, made threatening gestures, shoved the girl into the building, shook his fist against the sky. The young lover stood completely motionless, the girl cried. Suddenly the man glanced down at his skinny hairy legs in bedroom slippers. He uttered another threat, which however lost its effect because his voice cracked. Just after that the door slammed shut. The young man just stood there, as before. After about five minutes he shook himself like someone who has just awakened, and he walked away with heavy steps.

Poor thing, the girl, crying her eyes out now. She undoubtedly thought that she had brought shame to the family; that she was the first who had done something so terrible, beyond all bounds.

Constanze saw herself standing in front of a mirror and looking for signs in her face; signs that would reveal to her mother how excited she was, or what a hot pounding she felt when Mozart took her in his arms, or even when she heard his footsteps in the hallway.

A petal fell from a bouquet of roses on the chest in the corner, and then another one and a third. Constanze was cold. She closed the window. Where was Sophie?

That was stupid of Sophie to say that she might die before Constanze. She was healthy, as healthy as one could be at seventy-four, still nimble on her feet, despite the shuffling. Her appetite was good, she hardly got winded on the stairs.

No, Sophie would put the death shroud on her and write letters to her boys. She owed it to her.

But where in the world was she now?

It was so still. Another rose petal fell.

Would Mozart even recognize her?

He certainly could not hold it against her that she did not have a tombstone erected for him. She was not afraid that he would reproach her for that. And now he would get the monument, and at a place where the whole town would pass by, not just a few cemetery visitors. What would he say to that? She herself had written to the Swedish Queen requesting a contribution to the monument.

Nissen's book was also a type of memorial, perhaps even more lasting than the one cast in bronze. She had contributed her part to it. My God, when she thought back, how much difficulty and aggravation she had had in arranging for all the publication details after Nissen's death.

Mozart would more likely be angry about the letters that were destroyed. He saved every scrap of paper, just like his father. He did not put them in order, never; the pieces of paper lay around. But neither did he ever throw anything away, nor did he tolerate her using a letter to start a fire. But he could not expect her to let strangers read letters like that. He would not have wanted his Constanze to be presented like that. If it were now, she probably would not burn anything; but at that time she was younger. The insults of Mozart's father and sister were still raw, and they had remained raw for a surprisingly long time. It was probably also a mistake to cross out passages in the letters. Then people would imagine worse things than had actually been written.

Basically, she should not care about it. But she did. The man from Munich who claimed to be Mozart's friend; what was his name? Peter Summer, no, Peter Winter.[49] The guy who wrote such bad things about her to father Mozart – the word "slut" was from him – he had died in the meantime. If Mozart should ever see him, Mozart would set him straight and not mince any words. But that was highly unlikely, since, if there is any justice at all, a person like that would not be allowed to enter

into heaven. Not he, who had tried to convince Mozart
that it would be better to get a mistress than to marry
Constanze. Such a person was certainly in the other
place, or at least in purgatory, and not just for a little
while. But who knows, the ways of the Lord are
inscrutable. 'Slut.' That was nasty, a dirty, low-down lie.
And simply because this man was dead did not mean she
would forget and forgive. No one could expect that of
her.

She of course knew what the Bible said: "Whoso-
ever shall smite thee on thy right cheek." ... But that
business with the other cheek, that was for saints. She
was not a saint.

Sophie came into the room in her nightgown, a
nightcap on her head.

"It's time we went to bed."

"You act as if someone would scold us if we stayed
up too late. No one can scold us anymore, don't you
know that? We can go to bed whenever we want to and
get up whenever we want to. At five in the morning or at
twelve noon. That's nobody else's business."

Sophie raised her hands. "But how would it look if
no one were up by noon!"

"I don't feel like doing what people expect of me
anymore. Our mother has been dead for almost forty
years."

"She always wanted the best."

"Everybody does. Now I too want the best for me.
You can go to bed. Nobody's stopping you."

"No, no. I'll stay up with you."

How that sounded. Saint Sophie, pray for us.

Actually, she wanted to be alone, with this stillness, the thick darkness in every corner, the weak beam of light on the faces of the Mozarts in the picture. Wolfgang looked at her in a friendly way, not condescendingly like Nannerl. And the father, he seemed today as if he were not so sure anymore about always being right. He was reflective in a different way and glad to have his violin to hold onto. She would have liked him that way. It would have been nice to sit next to a person like that, to spoil him, to make something good for him to eat.

Above them all stood the mother, exactly in the middle. How much she looked like her son, or he like her, the forehead, the eyes, the mouth. She would not have been so harsh as the father. Whether she would have embraced the woman whom her son loved? Certainly. And everything would have been different. No, not everything, but lots of things.

"I would have liked to meet his mother," said Constanze.

"She could be your daughter now," said Sophie. "How old was she when she died?"

"Sixty-five."

"What a mix-up in heaven," said Sophie. "Or do you think that we'll all be young again?"

"I don't know."

"I think I would like to be twenty-two."

"But then you wouldn't know Haibl. You were much older when you saw him for the first time."

Sophie laid a finger on her nose. "Twenty-two, but with everything that happened afterwards. No, not everything, only the things that I like to remember."

"But then you wouldn't be twenty-two. At twenty-two you had only the experiences that you had had by then."

Sophie looked hurt. "You always have to spoil it for a person."

"I mean only if you want to count carefully."

"And how old do you want to be? In heaven, I mean?"

Constanze thought, shrugged her shoulders several times. "I don't think I would want to be any younger. Just have younger legs and joints. Otherwise everything I learned in the meantime would be for nothing." She shook herself. "What nonsense we're talking."

Sophie would not stop. "I bet you too would want to be under thirty, you just won't admit it. Then you wouldn't have any trouble, I mean, finally.... Or do you think that you can have two men over there?"

Constanze stood up, went over to the window and looked out at the church tower that stood out against the sky. If there was anything that had made Nissen's death easier for him, then it was the prospect of meeting Mozart. There was no doubt about it. Nissen's only regret would be that he could not tell the world what he would find out then. In case there were discussions there, with conversation back and forth. Regret – was regret admissible in heaven? She was irritated at Sophie who had led her thoughts in that direction, an idle direction, maybe even sinful. She had never thought about such things before. What was this supposed to be? I will know soon, she thought, so what is the point of speculating?

"Sorry," said Sophie. "I don't know what's the matter with me. Maybe it's because of the punch. But you have to admit it; we know a lot more people on the other side than we do here. I always wonder how it is there, whether there isn't a huge crowd, and how they all get along with one another. Whether there isn't a fight when, for example, father Mozart meets your Nissen and reproaches him about the letters...."

"And Nissen reproaches him that he always presented me so poorly in public."

"And Mozart joins them and says that all of that isn't important. They should listen instead to the wonderful piano that Saint Peter put on his cloud. Of course it could have a fuller tone, but then it would be too heavy for the cloud."

"I wonder whether they perform operas, or only sacred music?" Constanze entered into the game, they laughed and imagined a performance of *The Magic Flute* with all the heavenly hosts.

"What do you suppose Mozart would have thought about our cousin Carl Maria?"[50] Sophie asked. Constanze did not want to commit herself.

Suddenly she was overcome by great sadness. Almost at the same moment Sophie wiped a tear of laughter from her eye and said seriously, "You know, when I think about all those who await us there, it seems increasingly lonely here."

Constanze would have liked to put her arm around her sister, but something held her back. "We are the leftovers," she said.

With each year there were fewer people who shared the past with them, and with each death notice the past became more brittle. Each death left behind a hole, through which a cold wind forced its way into the present. Present – what was that? The room here, the way to the church, and, at most, the way to the cemetery. The world had become smaller and smaller. Inconceivable that she had at one time traveled to Denmark, to Milan. The people who made maps did not have any idea. They acted as if distances remained the same, as if anything at all remained the same on earth. Everything moved incessantly on and carried people along with it. All of them. She was happy for every letter, indeed. Each letter helped to prevent the walls of the house from closing in and crushing her. As strange as it sounded, even the way to the next room could be long and the breathing space narrow. She did not understand it herself, but that is how it was.

Sophie sat completely motionless. Constanze knew she struggled with the same fear, but that fear was not divisible. It was better not to talk about it. A superstitious dread held her back, as if the fear would increase with each word. Many years ago she had wanted to die, to be dead like him. She had really wished it on that winter morning, which she did not want to think about now, but which popped up again and again, especially recently. Fragments of memory streamed out of the shadows, and it did not help when she lighted all the lamps.

She could not, like Mozart, regard death as "*the* key *which unlocks the door to our true happiness*," as "*the true goal of our existence*." She had not "*formed such close relations with this best and truest friend of mankind, that his image is not only no longer terrifying to me, but is indeed very soothing and consoling!*" He was thirty-one when he wrote that, still had five years to live, still had *Don Giovanni* to write, as well as symphonies, string quartets, *Cosi fan tutte*, *The Magic Flute*, *La clemenza di Tito*, and the *Requiem*. There was certainly a difference whether a person was thirty-one or seventy-nine when he or she lay down and thought that "*I may not live to see another day*."

It was not death that she feared but rather dying. Sometimes she wished she had it behind her. But then she would see a ray of sunshine move across the bedspread, smell the aroma of coffee, hear the bells and the birds outside, hear Sophie's steps, and then she would want to live. To live with a passion that she herself did not understand. Only live. Only not have to die right now. Tomorrow. The day after tomorrow. But not today. First read Wowi's next letter. First enjoy the veal roast that one could smell through the whole house. First go to Hagenauer's Variety Shop and buy lavender for the drawers. Hagenauer had better lavender than the women at the market, and lavender kept away the moths. Was that important? What did she care if the moths built a nest in the drawers after she was gone?

out her hand and laid it on
and lay there lightly, cool and dry.
here," said Constanze.
at I'm here. I don't like to think
now down there in Diakovár."
happy there?"
· shoulders and let them drop.
d his position as choir director.
without him? The sexton looks
can think about him just as well
an, may God bless him."
wife to him too."
er head, and the ruffles on her
sorry that I met him so late, too
late to have children.

"But you weren't so old."

"Listen, I was forty and he forty-five."

Of course. Constanze always forgot that even little Sophie got older.

How Sophie had carried Wowi around as a tiny baby. How she talked to him before he could even say a word. How she sang to him, showed him his little hands and feet, rolled the fine hair on his head into a curl around her finger. How she told him what she had seen on the way from the outskirts of town to Rauhenstein Street. How she played ball and hide-and-seek with Carl, how she built houses with blocks and empty spools of thread, how they went for walks hand in hand. Both boys lit up when Sophie entered the room, always in haste. "Do you remember how you taught Carl to dance?"

"Of course. It would happen sometimes that he stepped on my foot, and then he would feel bad. He promised to marry me when he grew up."

"You see, he didn't get married because Haibl carried you off."

"Of course. That must be the reason."

The church clocks struck midnight, first one, then the other, then the third. Constanze always resolved to notice which was first, the Cathedral or St. Michael's or the Franciscan Church. The clocks could never agree on a common time. Maybe they had been set on the same day, one a little ahead, another a little behind, and thus the chiming remained staggered.

Sophie stood up resolutely. "I'm tired. I'm going to bed now." Constanze remained seated as Sophie kissed her on her forehead and then bent down to receive a kiss on the cheek. Since standing up was so difficult, Constanze did not like it when anyone watched her, not even Sophie.

The water in the pitcher on the bedside table was still lukewarm. Constanze washed her hands and face, rinsed her mouth out with water. The glass had been a gift from Carl, on the day of his departure for Livorno. Since then she had used it every evening and every morning and had always washed and dried it herself. Servant girls were often rather careless. The longer Carl was gone the more important the glass became to her. She had even taken it along to Denmark, since she simply could not bring herself to leave it behind with the other things in Vienna. Nissen had smiled and warned her not to forget that the glass was only a glass. She should be careful to avoid indulging in superstitions.

Yes, Carl, she thought as she carefully put the glass back on the table and did not allow her fingers to tremble. I have managed to keep the glass.

How difficult it had become to undress. She struggled with every button. Why could the seamstress not make the buttonholes bigger? They were much too small. But a bigger buttonhole would mean a few extra stitches.

Maybe she was being unfair.

One cannot always be fair. No one could. Sophie had often offered to help her with undressing. But it was not that bad yet. Not nearly that bad.

The bed rattled as Constanze lay down. Shortly thereafter the cabinet creaked, then a board in the hall.

The objects preserved her memories.

Her left shoulder hurt. With great effort she turned over on her side, but that did not help either. On her back, after all. The pillow was too high. No, too flat. I'm already like Pizzipankerl when he was old. He could not find any position to sleep in either. He pawed the pillow with his stiff legs, growled and turned around and around until he finally lay down with a sigh. Real barking had long been beyond his capacity.

"In the name of the Father, the Son, and the Holy Ghost. Amen. Our Father ... now and at the hour of our death. Amen."

She lay there as if on a deathbed with her hands

folded on her chest. "Holy Virgin, Mother of God, grant
that my good sister Sophie be with me then. Don't let me
die alone. Tomorrow I'll bring a nice big candle to the
Franciscan Church. A real wax candle."

"We flee to your shelter and refuge, Holy Mother of
God. Do not disdain our supplication in the hour of our
need...."

Her breathing became more regular, accompanying
the rhythm of the prayer. "Lord, bless and protect my
dear sons, Carl and Wolfgang. Grant them well-being on
earth. Grant all my dear ones who have passed on eternal
rest, and may perpetual light shine upon them. May they
rest in peace. Vouchsafe them eternal joy in the land of
the living, and may I be united with them in the blessed
life of the saints. Through our Lord, Jesus Christ, Thy
Son."

She crossed herself, pulled the blanket up to her
chin. Tomorrow she would go to the Franciscan Church.
The Madonna with the restrained smile made it easy to
trust. Constanze loved the small chubby angel who held
a mirror up for the Holy Virgin. Little angels were like
her dead children, and all so joyous in their golden
clouds. Mary however sometimes looked sad, although
one did not realize it upon first walking into the church.
But she never looked stern, no never.

"Let me live tomorrow so that I can bring you a
candle."

Not only for that reason.

The pale shadow by the window, what was it?
Constanze's heart beat faster and faster until it hurt. It

was the curtain. Only the curtain, caught on the window bar.

All at once she wanted to see the portrait, the unfinished one that lay in a box in the wardrobe. She got up out of bed. The floor was cold under her bare feet.

The door of the wardrobe stuck, as always in the fall. The damp air was to blame. Constanze pulled and tugged, braced herself against the other doorframe. When the door finally gave way she nearly fell over. She stood for a few minutes breathing heavily before she knelt down to pick up the box. She could not bend down or she would lose her balance completely.

She opened the box, took out the portrait. Then she had to get up on her feet again. She braced herself with her right hand against the middle casing of the wardrobe while holding the picture against herself with her left arm. On the third try she succeeded in getting up. She lighted the lamp on the bedside table, laid the picture in front of it. The flame flickered, light and shadow flittered around the blond hair, the high forehead. The light played on the clear wood until she believed to see Mozart's hands dancing on the piano.

What a shame that Lange had not completed the portrait. No, it was not a shame, not at all.

Why should Aloysia's husband have understood Mozart better than other people? He had simply looked, and perhaps precisely because he had not finished it, one could sense something of Mozart when one gazed at the picture. Above all she felt the desire to stroke his cheeks, his hair. The Novellos had sensed his genius as they respectfully stood there in front of it.

Mozart had written her "*that every night before going to bed I talk to your portrait for a good half hour
and do the same when I awake.*" She could not talk to
his portrait, could only look. And the longer she looked,
the greater became the sorrow in her. She would have
liked to ask, who are you after all? She would not have
gotten an answer, she knew that at least. Maybe he
would have kissed her or said something funny. She had
not seen his sorrow as he slept next to her every night.
Did he hide it from her? But not from Lange? Not even
when he talked about his apprehensions of death had she
comprehended his sorrow. At one time she even thought
that that was the just reward for eating the fat capon so
late at night in the "Silver Snake."

She could not take it back. A person cannot take
anything back, cannot change anything. Said is said. The
mind could, however, bend the memories into place,
bend them carefully as a goldsmith bends an ornament.
Thus one could gradually get the things into a shape that
did not hurt so much. Alternatively one could close the
door and turn the key twice in the lock. Not think about
it anymore. Then the matter would be buried, embalmed
like the emperor in his vault. Then nothing could change
because no air could get at it.

But how was it in Pompeii? There the bodies that
had been fully preserved for a thousand years or more
disintegrated into dust when the covering of ashes was
removed. Maybe that was the end, when the memory
disintegrated, when only dust particles remained, and

they could be blown away. It would not hurt anymore then.

The flame flickered, for the wick was too long. Actually, she should cut it, but she did not feel like going out to the other room and getting a pair of scissors, really not. Besides, the flickering was pleasant in a curious way, although it made her sort of sick to stare into the light; dizzy like after a fast dance. No, more like when her father twirled her around, so many years ago. But it was much too cold now to be sitting around, and especially with bare feet. She got into bed, put the picture on top of the blanket, bracing it against her knee. The expression looked different in the shadow. It became severe, more severe than she had ever seen him. Severe and strange and very far away.

Resolutely she took the picture and put it on the nightstand. She blew out the candle and settled down. Why should she be concerned about the past, the reproaches of some person or another yesterday, today, tomorrow?

The down blanket was light and warm, the finest white down, and the sheet was smooth damask that felt good. Sleep would come soon, it was already standing in the doorway. She walked with feather-light big steps on ground as soft as the clouds, and her arms spread out wide.

Long before she knew what the noise was – the crack, bang, boom – she sat up in bed.

Sophie came immediately, a candle in her hand, with her mouth half open and her nightcap perched crookedly on her head. "What in the world...?"

Mozart's portrait lay on the floor next to the night-stand with its face down.

Sophie picked up the portrait, put it in the wooden box, and closed the cover, all without saying a word. A few minutes later she asked Constanze if she needed anything.

"No, nothing. Sleep well."

"You too."

Upon closing the door Sophie permitted herself a slight sigh.

Constanze stared into the darkness. Scaring Sophie like that. It was not right. You just do not do that.

Her heart beat heavily against her chest. Her breath scratched her throat as if she had been running. With an unconscious movement she placed the fingers of her right hand on her left wrist and began to take her pulse.

Suddenly she was there again. This monstrous rage – it overcame her just as it had then. Her hands formed fists and she hit into the pillow. She almost screamed and could hardly hold herself back. But she did not want to see Sophie now. She would have to settle this with herself, no, with Mozart.

He had left her, had simply sneaked off into death and left her alone and helpless with a bawling infant and a disturbed seven-year-old. He escaped into death, just as he had often escaped into a joke, into a caress. Simply lay there with his pale, turgid face, not answering, letting her cry, leaving her alone with her despair, with her fear, with the debts, with the questions that she herself asked and the questions that others asked of her. Each question fed her rage. How could he do that to her, he who always claimed to love her? He had it good, no one bothered him. She hated her mother; hated Josefa, Schikaneder,[51] van Swieten, Albrechtsberger,[52] Puchberg, Joseph Deiner;[53] hated all those who took her hand and shook it as if it belonged to them, who mumbled inaudible phrases about God's will and divine providence. She hated the canary that began to chirp, hated the whining children, hated all who were alive, who came and went, hated her own fists pounding on the pillow, her twitching legs.

She was not sure that she had not hit Carl when he began to cry. Then her mother took him to her place, or maybe it was somebody else, she did not care. No, it was her mother who used to carry Wowi around in her arms. Then the house was empty all of a sudden, roaring with emptiness. Only Sophie came over to her with quiet steps, took her in her arms and cried with her, although Sophie did not know anything about her rage. Sophie cried silently, helped her out of her clothes, took away the pillow that was wet with Mozart's perspiration. Constanze struggled for it, but Sophie took it and brought her a new one, freshly ironed and cool. She covered her up.

The rage had been repressed all through the intervening years. Now it shook her as in a fit. The harder she tried to lie still the more her legs twitched, knocking against each other. She crammed a clenched fist into her mouth and bit down. It didn't hurt.

All at once she saw herself from the outside, saw herself lying there, a haggard white-haired woman who cried tears that were fifty years old. A fifty-year-old helpless rage burned in her throat as if she had drunk acid.

Earlier the rage had been followed by a long period of total indifference. She let everything happen to her, and it didn't matter. Anything and also its opposite was all right as long as she didn't have to make any decisions.

She saw the living room at Rauhenstein Street as if it were on a stage, highly reduced, roughly only twice the size of a dollhouse. But everything was there, the mirror in the golden frame, the chandelier, the two couches, even the porcelain figurines. She saw herself sitting on a chair, saw Carl come in and hug her, rubbing his head on her shoulder. She saw herself stand up abruptly, saw Carl's head hit the edge of the chair, saw how he stood there dazed and then began to cry, huge shiny tears like glass beads.

But now she mourned with the child, for the child. Earlier she was glad when van Swieten took the boy along to live in Prague. She could not stand his affection, every touch was terrible for her, she even loathed Wowi.

You had it easy, she said half out loud in the dark room. The sound of her own voice was frightening. She was certainly not crazy. Old, but not crazy.

She had managed her life well. She had paid the debts, all of them, even those to Puchberg. She had administered the estate and had seen to it that Nissen's biography was completed and published. What more could be expected of her?

Mozart had bequeathed his melodies to the world, his operas, his symphonies, his concerti, his masses, his chamber music, the arias that he wrote for other women. To her he had bequeathed his debts and two dependent children.

She was startled. I'm committing a sin, she thought. Have mercy, dear God.

A heavy weariness spread itself out in her body. Her head was strangely light and yet lay big like a balloon on the pillow. Images whirled through her head, the sunsprinkled grass under the giant beech tree in the Prater. She knew that she had stood there with Mozart, but she could not see him, only the whirling sun spots. She felt a desire like never before to see him, how he stood next to her, short, slight, in his silk-embroidered coat. At that time he still carried the gold watch, which he then gave to her at their wedding. She had not specified which of their sons should inherit the watch upon her death. They would have to settle that between themselves.

She reached for the watch on the nightstand and let the chain ripple through her fingers. She ran her finger around the curve, a comforting feeling in her hand.

Forgive me, she thought. You will forgive me, won't you? You always forgave me, just as I always forgave you. Beginning with that stupid occasion when I let the calves of my legs be measured by some cavalier at Baroness Waldstätten's place. I don't even know anymore who it was. How was I supposed to know that that was not proper for a marriageable girl? I always just watched what other people did and I did the same. What I learned at home wasn't valid for the outside world, do you understand? I always complied as much as I could. How was I supposed to know with whom I should comply and with whom not? Especially since she was the Baroness. I would also have complied with the wishes of your father and your sister, believe me. I could have done it, for I was very good at complying, but they didn't want it. They didn't give me the chance to learn from them. I can believe that some people are something in themselves, but not I. I was always only a mirror. Is a mirror responsible for what it reflects?

It is written that a wife should follow her husband, is it not? Just a few weeks ago the Father gave a sermon about that. I don't know his name, it was the one who stutters. But you, of course, don't know him. He seems to me to be an old man, but you can't possibly know him. He was probably still in school when you....

I never would have thought that I could talk to you. Once again, I mean. Only I don't get an answer. Sometimes, you know, sometimes I think if only I had better ears I would be able to hear the answers in your music. Is it my fault that my ears are too coarse? It's obvious that yours were different from those of ordinary people. That's the reason my Nissen made a drawing of them. A good drawing, I think.

And if you look at Wowi's ears, they're shaped exactly the same. Thus you shouldn't pay any attention to the idle rumors some people spread. As if I and some "silly chap...." You said that, do you remember? And that he's an idiot. How is an idiot supposed to....

No, really not. I never talk like that. Honestly. I speak in a dignified way, and even such refined folks as the English gentleman and lady confirmed that. I speak as befits the widow of a State Councilor. You would laugh, for sure. I learned that after our time together. If I had known at the time what I know now, then we would have been better off, I swear. Financially, I mean. Then I would have handled all the negotiations with your commissioners and with the theaters. I would have been your agent. You wouldn't have had to give music lessons to the young women students and would have had time for composition. Or would you have missed the young women?

I included the poor Mozart woman, your cousin, in my will. That must be to your liking, isn't it? You shouldn't think that I want everything only for myself. I forget sometimes that I'm now a wealthy woman. One forgets everything when one gets old. Of course you can't understand that. You were never old.

Would you still have liked me with my wrinkles and the flabby skin on my arms and stomach? Would you still have said "Stanzi Marini" to me?

Stanzi Marini.

A feeling of warmth circulated in her, trickled down to the tips of her toes. They were so far down. Miles away. Her hands too.

A melody went through her head, one of his, but she did not know which work it was from. She hummed silently to herself until she got to a high note which she could not reach even in her thoughts.

You're not mad at me, are you, because I told Nissen that I felt more attracted to your musical ability than I did to you as a person?

What was I supposed to tell him? I mean, he revered you so much anyway. You can't imagine it, but you never had a more ardent admirer. He wanted to know everything about you. I would never have been able to answer a lot of his questions, not even today. But, you know, I thought too that he would probably be jealous. You knew how it really was anyway, and it's nobody else's business. He had to have something too that was his own, you know. And when he appeared on the scene, then your music really was more important. But it was always more important for you too, so how could you be irritated by what I said? And with him it was never as it had been with you, so much laughter and joy. He was always serious, very dignified. He never laid aside his dignity throughout all those years. Look at his portrait. It's really quite good. There you can see how he was. A good man, there's no one better. And a good father too for Carl and Wowi. Don't take offense, but you yourself couldn't have been a better father than he. Out of sheer joy that Carl gave me a wedding gift of coral earrings, he reimbursed Carl for the cost of transportation, five ducats, and also the more than thirty-five gulden that we had paid for copying, customs, and so on. Simply from that you can see how he was, very loving toward me, as if caring for a memento.

She realized all of a sudden that she was talking to

herself. Mozart was out of reach.

But she still knew where he was ticklish. Grant him eternal rest, o Lord, and may perpetual light shine upon him.

She was a respectable woman. When the English people in Gastein insisted on bathing in the nude, she declined and waited instead for two hours for her beloved bath. Nor had she worn the transparent dresses that were very fashionable, especially in France, although with her figure, she could have worn them well. Those women looked more naked than naked. No wonder that godlessness was so prevalent and that the revolutionaries killed each other off.

There was no equality in the world. That was not included in the plan of creation. Inequality was the order of the day. One had to adjust to that and find one's place as well as possible. The good Nissen always said.... What did he say? It escaped her, but it was wise, and right. She could not imagine equality. What was equal in the world at all? Not even her two hands.

How her veins protruded, somewhat more to the right than to the left. It was a strange feeling to run your fingers along them. Sophie must cut her nails tomorrow. She could do that much better than Luise.

Mozart had longed for liberty, liberty to compose music. But that was a different kind of liberty from what the revolutionaries dreamed of. Or not? The arrogance of the high lords made him furious, so furious that he literally boiled over. Just the thought of Count Arco![54] What all had Mozart not called the Prince-Archbishopric

Chief Chamberlain, and even the Prince-Archbishop himself. "Arch-idiot" was still harmless enough. Was liberty the opposite of obedience, or more? Mozart had indeed learned to obey, learned it thoroughly. Even long after he had renounced obedience to his father in reality, he still signed his letters with "Your Most Obedient Son." That was not a lie after all, since Leopold Mozart had only the one son, whether obedient or not.

Liberty – she said the word several times over, half out loud. The *L* vibrated on her palate. Strange, how the *T* made her aware that she had a tongue.

"Liberty."

She shook her head. She had always had difficulty with big words. She preferred to leave them for other people who could deal with them.

But she was thinking altogether too much today. Much too much.

What was the third thing? Fraternity. The fraternal brothers should worry about that if they wanted to.

Had the evening meal been too heavy after all? Tomorrow Luise should buy a soup bone. A thick soup with vegetables and marrowbone dumplings, with lots of parsley and a pinch of nutmeg, that would be just the thing. Of course, Luise would not get the taste just right, as Josefa or her mother had done. Her mouth watered still today when she thought of their good cooking. Mother's face when she was doing the seasoning – how she rubbed the herbs between her fingers. Then the corners of her mouth did not turn down, then her severe lips changed to mellow. She looked gentle, and when she blew on a spoonful before tasting, it was as if she were going to kiss someone, very tenderly.

Sometime, almost a hundred years ago, she must have looked at Constanze's father like that.

To compare her father to a pot of soup: was she already losing her mind? Already? After all, she was almost eighty. She could lose it if she wanted to. Actually, she could do whatever she wanted to, she did not have to give an account to anybody. But it was not so easy to know what it was she really wanted. Since Nissen's death there was no one to tell her what she should want.

She was so grateful to him, honestly and sincerely grateful for everything that he had done for her and even more for everything that he had taught her. The years in Copenhagen were good. She thought of the rich merchant who named his son Mozart out of pure reverence. Petersen was his name. Who says then, if you please, that her memory was failing? She still remembered even the name. Copenhagen. When she appeared at the opera with Nissen all heads turned to see her. The Most Gracious Queen, Her Majesty Maria Sophie Friederike, had graciously spoken with her more than once and had expressed her veneration for Mozart. And Nissen stood at her side, modest and dignified, smiling with his eyes. The good Nissen. He always knew exactly what was proper at the time, what deportment was appropriate for a particular occasion.

Oh yes, now she remembered what had gone through her mind, so fleetingly that she could hardly recognize the melody: *Se vuol ballare, signor contino*. Not the aria, actually, just the overture where the theme first appeared.

Nissen never particularly liked the aria, it was too inflammatory for him. Maybe he was right. Certainly he was right. Order must be present in the world, as in music too. Mozart liked the aria though. And the way Benucci[55] sang it at the premier performance, as if he meant every word. Suddenly she saw Mozart in front of her, in the red dress-coat that he liked to wear, but with a fez on his head and a whip in his hand. His face was completely in the shadow, and in front of him was Count Arco, hopping around like a giant dancing bear. She had never seen the Prince-Archbishopric Chief Chamberlain, but she knew it was he. He comically lifted his left leg, then his right leg, and Mozart snapped the whip. Constanze burst out laughing.

The Storace woman did not bother her. Whenever she thought of Figaro, Susanna, of course, inevitably appeared as well. She walked in with a light step, as if she had wings on her heels, skipping, curious, impatient. Always in breathless expectation. No one would have taken her for a married woman. She herself, however, Constanze, waddled like a duck at the time. Little Leopold had hit and kicked with his arms and legs in her abdomen, wilder than all her other babies. Later he died from convulsions. Not even a month old.

All of the difficulties of pregnancy, the danger, the pain of giving birth – and even then it was too early to be glad. Danger was lurking everywhere. The children died, of fever, of convulsions, of some illness or another. Or they were simply extinguished. No one knew why, and once again a little casket was carried out. How are you supposed to learn to love when everything goes by so quickly? You were afraid to become attached.

Maybe she just did not have the talent for it. Maybe you had to have a talent for love, just as for music, mathematics, or drawing.

What was the story about the buried talents? Did not he who buried his talent get cast into outer darkness, where there shall be weeping and gnashing of teeth?

Had she buried her talent?

She was only a woman, indeed. After all, she had made her husband happy, had she not?

She hummed Kontanze's aria from the *Abduction*: "Oh, in loving I was happy."

Had she been happy? For sure, happy twice-over, two good husbands. Both of them loved and cherished her. That was what she should have told Sophie.

Two good husbands, two good sons. What more could a woman want?

Two good sons. Carl bore his name with less difficulty. For a government official it did not make so much difference. But she had no idea how hard it must have been for him definitively to give up his hopes of a career as a musician. And Wowi? He seemed tired and worn out at his last visit. There was not much life in him. Where had his courage gone? He could compose music but he did not have to. Was that the difference?

She had written to both of them, "*that neither of*

Mozart's sons should be mediocre so as not to earn for himself more shame than honor." Had the fear of mediocrity taken the wind out of their sails? Had she demanded too much, was she too impatient, and did she thus hinder their development? Had she thought of her sons at all as she forced her conceptions on them? Only God knew. He knew too that she had done what she felt to be right at the time.

Forgive us our trespasses, as we forgive those who trespass against us.

Why could she not leave it at that? Why did she have to examine her life today as if it were a ledger?

Was it really a lie when she told the people who came and asked her about Mozart what they wanted to hear? It did not hurt him when she told them that he was an enthusiastic nature lover. Why should people not imagine him as they wanted him to be, if that helped them enjoy his music more?

It would have made precious little difference to him, she knew that for sure.

She sat up in bed. Sleep was out of the question anyway, and her shoulder hurt more and more.

Everyone had an image of him, and everyone wanted to hear which of the images was the most accurate. How was she supposed to know, after all these years? Did not even the features of a dead person change? Besides, all the images were stationary, they captured a fixed moment; whereas Mozart was never stationary, he was constantly in motion. Was it then so important whether his nose was attached in this way or that, whether his eyebrows were raised one way or another? His double chin, which he enjoyed so much having scratched, they did not want to hear about that.

The images were to blame for the fact that she could not see him anymore. Her memories clearly showed everything around him but left out his face, she thought. His face has been talked to pieces, dissolved into words, nothing but words.

Now they were erecting a monument for him. She was happy about that. But he, what would he have said to that? He who did not like to play for an audience that did not understand music.

He did not need any of us, she murmured. Not any of you and not me either. Not there, where it really counts. There he needed only his music. Even if he wrote: "*You cannot imagine how I have been aching for you all this long while. I can't describe what I have been feeling – a kind of emptiness, which hurts me dreadfully – a longing, which is never satisfied, which never ceases, and which persists, nay rather increases daily. When I think how merry we were together at Baden – like children – and what sad, weary hours I am spending here! Even my work gives me no pleasure, because I am accustomed to stop working now and then and exchange a few words with you. Alas! this pleasure is no longer possible. If I go to the piano and sing something out of my opera, I have to stop at once, for this stirs my emotions too deeply. Basta! The very hour after I finish this business I shall be off and away from here.*"

She should have gone right back to Vienna when

she received that letter. Then it would...

Nothing would. That emptiness, that yearning, she could not have filled it. Not she and not anybody else. Nobody. During the past one or two years she sometimes sensed a feeling of that emptiness. But perhaps it was a different one.

If only it were day. Then Sophie would come in and say something, anything, and it would break the silence.

Konstanze's aria went through her head again.

"... and he rested on my bosom."

Yes, he had rested on her bosom. Was that enough? It had to be enough.

Soon no one would bear the name Mozart anymore, that distinction, that burden. The name would die out with Wolfgang and Carl.

They said that he was immortal. Grillparzer[56] would allegedly write a poem or had already written one for the ceremony of the unveiling of the monument. But that monument cannot be invited as a dinner guest.

The small thin man, who could leap over tables and chairs and turn somersaults meowing like a cat, who made a fool of himself – or of the others? (the thought occurred to her, to her own surprise) – this man would stand honorably and motionlessly on the square. But it would not be the one who wrote *Figaro* and *Don Giovanni*. It would be a statue and, like all images, tell more about the one who created it than about the one it represented. Wowi and Carl would come to the celebration. Maybe Wowi would conduct his father's *Requiem* again like after Nissen's death. They all said at the time that they had never heard the death mass played so beautifully or so movingly before.

Wowi had loved Nissen like a father. At least she had accomplished that as a mother: giving her son a father.

A pity that he never went to England, despite the cordial invitation of the Novellos. In England one would have welcomed a Mozart with open arms. Finally, perhaps, it was precisely that which held him back. He would, of course, have been received as a son. Was it a mistake to make him into a Wolfgang? Would he have had an easier life as Franz Xaver Wolfgang Mozart?

Thoughts at night. Idle night-thoughts. It would not be much longer until it got light, and she would make strong coffee. Mona should get some fresh rolls. No, not Mona, she had been gone a long time. Luise. Naturally, Luise. Funny that the servant had the same name as her sister Louise, next to whom she felt like a servant herself.

Luise should finally polish the silverware. Constanze had noticed yesterday that the forks and spoons were tarnished, unsightly, as if they were not pure silver. She would tell her as soon as she got up. Indeed, she, Constanze von Nissen, widow of Mozart, Weber by birth, possessed six silver spoons, six silver forks, and five silver soup spoons. It would be six if one had not been inadvertently thrown out with the garbage. Fifty years ago the entire tableware was in the pawn shop. She would still like to know today who had kept the pawn ticket. Mozart, of course, did not pay attention to any of that. Who would wear her good pearls when she was not here anymore? Wowi could not give them to his Josephine. Her husband would become suspicious, even in spite of all his blind faith or indifference. And in the meantime, was that love not a thing of the past?

The sky was not dark anymore, but not light either. In contrast to the darkness in the room, the window stood out. A dog barked, only once and somewhat hoarsely. The earliest domestic servants would soon be on their way. She shook out her pillow and lay down again. Now she could fall asleep, she was suddenly very tired. One or two hours, no more, otherwise Sophie would begin to question. The outlines of the furniture stood out like silhouettes. Wowi and Carl would sell most of it, the transportation to Vienna or to Milan would certainly be too expensive. And the things here had no history for them, only for her. It made her feel sad that her things would end up at some second-hand store; fingered by strangers, to whom the scratch on the table top would say nothing of the day when the knife slipped as she was trimming a quill for Nissen; in whose eyes this scratch was only a mar that reduced the value; for whom the round spot was only a blemish, not a remembrance of a happy evening.

Who now slept in the bed in which her children were born, in which Mozart died? When you had lived as long as she, you did not leave many people behind, but for that, all the more things. That had not occurred to her when she moved to Copenhagen with Nissen.

Where actually was the mirror with the gold frame? She had certainly taken it along to Denmark.

What disorder in her head, unimportant things randomly mixed together with important ones, exactly as it was before in the house on Rauhenstein Street. She tried to recall the fugue that Mozart had written for her. Fugues represented supreme order, an artistic form in which confusion has no place. The fugue escaped her, she could not even recall the theme. Instead, the Papageno-Pamina duet unexpectedly went through her mind. "Man and wife, wife and man, Rise to join in God's great plan."

Then she must have dozed off, for she was suddenly startled as the room resounded with the ring of church bells, and cool gray light shone in. She was surprised that she was not exhausted after a night like that, but rather remarkably awake and looking forward to the day. The aroma of coffee streamed from the kitchen. Constanze lifted her legs out of bed, rinsed out her mouth and combed her hair. An old woman does not have to go around looking tousled, as well as wrinkled. That is no happy sight, she always said. That was not vanity but rather consideration for others.

She went to the window and opened it. A single watery beam of sunlight danced on the square. Down there is where Mozart would stand, a beautiful, dignified monument. That was what they all said who had seen the statue in Munich. Whether it was alright with him that he stood with his back turned to them? Presumably he would just shrug his shoulders. That is not me anyway. And probably add that he was looking forward to the sparrows and pigeons who sooner or later impinge upon the stiff dignity of any monument. They invent you, she said inaudibly. The greatest son of your beloved hometown is what they call you now. Do you find that amusing? They invent you as they want to have you. I cannot do that. But I cannot find you anymore either.

She inhaled the morning air, felt the coolness and freshness penetrating deeply into her lungs. It was good to be alive. She looked forward to walking to the square later and watching the workers, to bringing the caretaker's dog a piece of sausage.

Sophie was talking to Luise in the other room.

Constanze started to laugh. Sophie flung open the door, stood there with a worried look on her face and asked: "What's going on? What's the matter? Aren't you feeling well?"

"I just thought of something," said Constanze. "I'll never again be able to imagine how he scratched himself, because then I would always have to think: so that's how a genius scratches himself. You see?" Sophie shook her head.

Constanze put her arms around her. "It doesn't matter. The air already tastes like snow. Try it."

Even if it was not like that, it is a fact that in 1841 an old woman often looked out in the rain at the square in Salzburg which was called Michaelis Plaza at the time and was later renamed Mozart Place.

Notes

1. Sophie Haibl, née Weber.
Born in 1767 in Zell am Wiesenthal, died in 1846 in Salzburg. Youngest sister of Constanze, married Petrus Jacob Haibl in 1807.
2. Luise NN.
Servant girl whom Constanze remembered in her will.
3. Carl Thomas Mozart.
Born on September 21, 1784, in Vienna, died on November 2, 1858, in Milan. Son of Wolfgang Amadeus Mozart and his wife Constanze, née Weber. After the death of his father, Carl was brought by van Swieten to Franz Gottfried X. Niemetschek in Prague. In 1797, before finishing school, he was sent to Livorno for a business apprenticeship. He moved to Milan in 1805, studied music there under Bonifazio Asioli, but gave up that course of study. He became a Royal and Imperial Prefect in the service of the Vice Chancellor of Naples. Constanze gave him his father's piano. He visited her a number of times in Salzburg and was present also for the unveiling of the Mozart monument in 1842. His daughter Constanze died in 1833.
4. Johann Georg Leopold Mozart.
Born in 1719 in Augsburg, died in 1787 in Salzburg. Composer, violinist, and musicologist. He studied philosophy and law in Salzburg, was expelled from the uni-

versity; obtained a position as second violinist and later as Deputy Music Director at the Prince-Archbishopric court. His book, *A Treatise on the Fundamental Principles of Violin Playing*, made him famous throughout Europe. He married Anna Maria Pertl in 1747. "The miracle that God brought to life in Salzburg" changed his life; and, to the detriment of his own career, he dedicated himself almost exclusively to the education of his children. He was at once father, teacher, advisor, publisher, copyist, secretary, travel agent, even valet to his son. He was upset by his son's break with the Prince-Archbishop and even more by his "mésalliance" with Constanze; he felt his son slipping away from his grasp. His despairing and futile attempts to hold onto his son were the tragedy of his later years.

Excerpt from the journal of Dominikus Hagenauer, May 28, 1787: "On Whit Monday, the 28th, the local Deputy Music Director Leopold Mozart died. He had brought great honor to Salzburg with the birth of his two children approximately twenty years ago.... The now deceased father was a man of great wisdom and prudence. Even apart from music, he would have been in a position to do great service for his country."

5. Raimund Leopold Mozart.
Born on June 17, 1783, died on August 19, 1783. Constanze's first child.

6. Johannes Thomas Mozart.
Born on Octobr 18, 1786, died on November 15, 1786.

Constanze's third child.

7. Franz Xaver Wolfgang (Wowi) Mozart.
Born on July 26, 1791, in Vienna, died on July 29, 1844, in Karlsbad. Constanze's sixth child and the second one to survive; renamed by his mother Wolfgang Amadeus. After the age of five he lived with the Duscheks in Prague and got his first piano lessons from Niemetschek. Later he studied in Vienna with Salieri, among others. Salieri ascertained a "rare talent for music" and predicted a career that would be "equal to that of his celebrated father." He went to Lemberg as a music teacher in 1808 and returned to Vienna in 1835. In 1841 he became Honorary Music Director of the Cathedral Music Association and Mozarteum in Salzburg; and in 1842 he became "Compositore onorario" of the Congregazione ed Accademia Santa Cecilia in Rome. He bequeathed "the manuscripts in his possession and the music fragments written personally by his famous father, a number of family papers, the portrait of his father and several other family portraits ... as well as his entire library to the Mozarteum as a lasting memorial to his father."

8. George Nicolaus Nissen.
Born in 1761 in Hadersleben, Denmark, died in 1826 in Salzburg. Danish diplomat, Constanze's second husband; a great admirer of Mozart and his third biographer.

9. Aloysia (Louise) Lange, née Weber.
Born in Zell am Wiesenthal in 1761, died in Salzburg in 1839. Second-oldest sister of Constanze. She "sings su-

perbly" and has "a beautiful, pure voice." Mozart fell intensely in love with her in Mannheim. He gave her lessons and made plans to travel with her and her father to Italy. She married the actor and painter Joseph Lange; separated from him, left Vienna and sang in Amsterdam, Paris, Frankfurt, and Zurich. Mozart composed many arias for her. She was the first Madame Herz in *Der Schauspieldirektor* and the original Donna Anna in the Viennese premier of *Don Giovanni*.

10. Prince-Archbishop Hieronymus Joseph Graf Colloredo, 1732-1812.

Prince-Archbishop of Salzburg, 1772-1803. Adherent of the Enlightenment, frugal and sober. He was convinced that he could enlist "hundreds who would serve him better than he [Mozart]."

11. Name of the house.

12. Johann von Thorwart.

He advanced from servant to box attendant at the Burg Theater; became checkroom officer, auditor of accounts and assistant to the financial director at the Royal and Imperial National Theater. The High Court Council named him guardian for the Weber daughters.

13. Letters are hereafter cited from the following edition: *The Letters of Mozart & His Family*, ed. and trans. Emily Anderson. 3 vols. (London: Macmillan, 1938).

14. Michael Puchberg, 1741-1822 .

Viennese businessman, principal creditor of the Mozarts.

15. Antonio Salieri.
Born in Legnago in 1750, died in Vienna in 1825. Composer, Court Music Director, and chamber musician in Vienna. As of 1775 his influence became noticeable in the entire music life in Vienna. He gave lessons to, among many others, Franz Xaver Wolfgang Mozart.
16. Carl Ditters von Dittersdorf.
Born in Vienna in 1739, died in Neuhof, Bohemia, in 1799. Composer and violinist.
17. Anna Maria Mozart.
Born and died on November 16, 1789, in Vienna. Constanze's fifth child.
18. Franz Hofdemel, ca. 1755-1791.
Chancery clerk in Vienna, Mozart's creditor. His wife was Mozart's pupil.
19. Karl Alois Johann Nepomuk Vinzenz Leonhard, Prince Lichnowsky, 1756-1814. Student and patron of Mozart, later patron of Beethoven. He invited Mozart to accompany him on a trip to Prague, Dresden, Leipzig, and Berlin.
20. The dotted passages are words that have been blotted out in the autograph.
21. Franz de Paula Hofer, 1755-1796.
Austrian violinist, friend of the Mozart family, husband of Josefa, née Weber.
22. Satmann, perhaps a copyist.
23. Johann Lorenz Hagenauer, 1712-1792.
Landlord and friend of Leopold Mozart. He financed the

trips with the two child prodigies to a large extent in advance. The "Variety Shop" [Spezereywarenhandlung] still exists, selling mainly teas and spices.

24. Mary Sabilla Novello, 1789-1854.

A talented, versatile, and energetic woman of German-Irish descent; center of a circle of writers, painters, and musicians. Together with her husband, Vincent, she undertook "A Mozart Pilgrimage" (the title of their diaries).

Vincent N. Novello, 1781-1861.

Organist, choir director, conductor, publisher, and composer; of Italian heritage. He was an enthusiastic admirer of Mozart, whom he called the "Shakespeare of music." In 1829, when the rumor spread that Maria Anna Mozart was completely impoverished and ailing, Vincent Novello took up a collection for her. Together with his wife, Mary, he traveled to Salzburg to deliver the honorary gift to "Nannerl." At the same time he collected material for a biography of Mozart, which was planned but never completed. The diaries of Vincent and Mary Novello were first published in London in 1955.

25. Maria Anna Walburga Ignatia ("Nannerl") Berchtold zu Sonnenburg, née Mozart.

Born on July 30 or 31, 1751, in Salzburg, died on October 29, 1829, in Salzburg. Pianist; celebrated as a child prodigy throughout Europe, together with her brother. After 1769 she stayed in Salzburg with her mother, later with her father, while her brother traveled. He praised her compositions, none of which is however extant. She was not allowed to marry the friend of her youth, d'Yppold, because he was not in a position to support a family. She was married to the widower Johann Baptist Baron von Berchtold zu Sonnenburg from St. Gilgen in 1784. After his death in 1801 she returned to Salzburg with her two children, Leopold Alois Pantaleon (1785-1840) and Johanna (1789-1805). She was much in demand as a piano teacher. She became blind in 1825.

26. Maria Elisabeth Baroness Waldstätten, 1744-1811.

Patron and friend of Mozart. She lived apart from her husband and seemed to enjoy her shady reputation.

27. Mona NN.

Servant girl; she accompanied Constanze on some of her numerous visits to the spa at Gastein.

28. Name of an inn.

29. Franz Georg Graf Walsegg-Stuppach, 1763-1827.

Music dilettante; he frequently gave commissions for compositions which he then claimed as his own. The *Requiem* was intended for the first anniversary of the death of his wife, Anna.

30. Gottfried van Swieten, 1730-1803.

Son of Gerard van Swieten, personal physician to the Empress Maria Theresia; Austrian diplomat, music lover. He was the one who first acquainted Mozart with the music of Bach and Handel; and he was the sole subscriber to a concert series that Mozart wanted to give in 1789. He made the arrangements for Mozart's funeral and brought Carl to Prague.

31. Josefa Duschek, 1754-1834.

Famous Bohemian singer, wife of Franz Xaver Duschek. Mozart wrote "Ah, lo previdi" and "Bella mia fiamma" for her.

32. Caterina Cavalieri, 1761-1801.

Singer in the Josephinian National Singspiel, pupil and friend of Salieri. She was the first Konstanze, the first Donna Elvira in Vienna, and the first Mlle. Silberklang.

33. Names have been crossed out by a later hand.

34. Franz Xaver Süssmayr, 1766-1803.

Austrian composer; pupil and admirer of Mozart, at the same time a pupil of Salieri.

35. Breitkopf & Härtel.

Music publishing firm, founded in 1719 in Leipzig.

36. Mechetti.

Music publisher and art dealer in Vienna.

37. Friedrich Schlichtegroll, 1765-1822.

Philologist, Mozart's first biographer.

38. Franz Xaver Niemetschek (Niemeszek), 1766-1849.

High school teacher in Prague, friend of the Mozart family, Wowi's first teacher; Mozart's second biographer.

39. Johann Heinrich Feuerstein.

Professor and medical doctor in Pirna near Dresden. He edited Nissen's biography of Mozart after Nissen's death

and wrote the foreword for it. He died in a state of
mental derangement.

40. Johann Anton André, 1775-1842.

Music publisher in Offenbach. Constanze sold him Mozart's unpublished works for three thousand one hundred
and fifty gulden. He compiled a thematic index of Mozart's manuscripts.

41. Fridolin Weber, 1733-1779.

Civil servant in Zell in Wiesenthal. At the urging of his
wife, Caecilia, he moved to Mannheim, where he worked
as bass, violinist, and prompter. To increase his income
he also worked as a copyist, and thus he met Mozart.

42. Joseph Haydn.

Born on March 3, 1732, in Rohrau, died on May 31,
1809, in Vienna. Composer, the first of the Viennese
classicists, fatherly friend to Mozart. Following is an excerpt from a letter of Haydn to the administrator Franz
Rott in Prague, dated December 1787: "I only wish I
could impress on every friend of music, and on great
men in particular, the same depth of musical sympathy,
and profound appreciation of Mozart's inimitable music,
that I myself feel and enjoy; then nations would vie with
each other to possess such a jewel within their frontiers.
Prague ought to strive to retain this precious man, but
also to remunerate him; for without this the history of a
great genius is sad indeed, and gives very little encour-
agement to posterity to further exertions, and it is on this
account so many promising geniuses are ruined. It en-

rages me to think that the unparalleled Mozart is not yet engaged by some imperial or royal court! Forgive my excitement; but I love the man so dearly!" [Cited from *Letters of Distinguished Musicians*, trans. Lady Wallace (London: Longmans, Green, and Co., 1867), p. 108].

43. Josefa Hofer, née Weber.

Born in Zell in Wiesenthal in 1759, died in Vienna in 1819. Singer, oldest sister of Constanze, the first Queen of the Night.

44. Caecilia Weber, née Stamm.

Born in Mannheim in 1727, died in Vienna in 1793. Constanze's mother. With rare unanimity she is described as terrible; only for Sophie she is "our good mother," who "became increasingly fond of Mozart, as he of her too."

45. Joseph Lange, 1752-1831.

Actor in Vienna, famous especially for his role as Hamlet; painter, friend of Mozart, husband of Aloysia, née Weber.

46. Petrus Jacob Haibl, 1762-1826.

Singer, composer, and choir director; husband of Sophie, née Weber.

47. Anna Selina (Nancy) Storace, 1766-1817.

English-Italian singer, the first Susanna in *Le nozze di Figaro*.

48. Johann Nepomuk Hummel, 1778-1837.

Pianist, composer, pupil of Mozart.

49. Peter (von) Winter, 1754-1825.

German composer; wrote *The Labyrinth*, which was
conceived as a continuation of *The Magic Flute*.
    50. Carl Maria (von) Weber, 1786-1826.
Romantic composer, conductor, pianist, and musicologist; cousin of Constanze.
    51. Emanuel (actually Johann Joseph) Schikaneder,
1751-1812.
Actor, theater director, singer, composer, dramatist, and
impresario; wrote the libretto for *The Magic Flute*, and
founded the "Theater an der Wien." A friend of the Mozart family since his guest performance in Salzburg in
1780.
    52. Johann Georg Albrechtsberger, 1736-1809.
Composer, teacher, musicologist, and organist. Mozart
insisted that Albrechtsberger was entitled to be his successor as organist at St. Stephen's Cathedral.
    53. Joseph Deiner.
Waiter in the restaurant, "Silver Snake," Mozart's factotum. He washed Mozart's corpse and clothed it in the
garments of the dead fraternity brothers.
    54. Karl Graf Arco, 1743-1830.
Chief Chamberlain to the Archbishop Colloredo. Count
Arco booted Mozart out after an argument with him in
the reception chamber of the Archbishop's palace. Mozart swore "to give him a kick in the pants, and to do it
in public."
    55. Francesco Benucci, 1745-1825.
Italian singer, the first Figaro, the first Leporello.

56. Franz Grillparzer, 1791-1872.
Austrian author, dramatist, Archival Director of the Finance Administration. He wrote a poem for the unveiling of the Mozart statue in Salzburg.

Afterword

In his famous biography of Wolfgang Amadeus
Mozart, Wolfgang Hildesheimer speaks of Mozart's
wife, Constanze, in terms of "depressing banality." That
seems to be the consensus among observers, from
Mozart's own father to present day biographers and play-
wrights. Welsh takes a different approach, allowing
Constanze to tell the story from her point of view. Fram-
ing the problem in her ironic subtitle, *An Unimportant
Woman*, Welsh shows that any valuation has at least two
sides; and further that ordinary life – however 'unimportant' – is worthy of representation.

Rather than a man, the musical genius, it is a
woman, his wife, who stands at the center. The book is
about gender differences to the extent that women were
– and still are – regarded as second-class citizens. Welsh
commented as follows on her motivation for writing the
book:

> Thinking about the situation, I find it
> deplorable. Here is a woman who is
> seventy-nine years old and who has been a

widow for fifty years. The only thing that anyone can say about her is that she, as a young girl, was married for eight years to a man whose greatness she of course did not recognize. People have reproached her for her compliance, which, on the other hand, has always been regarded as the cardinal feminine virtue.

To call the book 'feminist' would not be appropriate, for, even apart from the anachronism, Welsh does not allow such polarities to arise. Rather than retrospective moral indignation over the role of women, the author shows how the protagonist comes to terms with her own 'marginality.'

The book is not only about a woman, but also about aging, another unpopular topic. "Living beyond the age of fifty is indecent, vulgar, immoral!" wrote Dostoevsky's underground diarist in his search for meaning in life. Welsh explores the debatability of that stance and comes to a different conclusion. The central question remains: What constitutes a worthy life? And Welsh finds dignity, selfhood, and a sense of fulfillment also in old age. Whereas most biographers and novelists focus on young people in the developmental or decisive stages of life, Welsh chose to portray a later period, when virtually all decisions have been made. The narrative voice is that of Mozart's widow, fifty years after his death, as she looks back on her life of nearly eighty years.

Constanze Mozart, née Weber (1762-1842), outlived her famous husband, Wolfgang Amadeus

Mozart (1756-1791), by over fifty years. The narrative is set in 1841, which serves as an anchor for the interwoven time levels of present, past, past perfect, and future perfect possibilities. There are many reflections of late eighteenth and early nineteenth-century life in Salzburg and Vienna and again Salzburg. Generous notes provide a historical framework for the many figures mentioned in the text. (The endnotes are the author's, the occasional footnotes are the translator's.) Further documentary is offered by excerpts from letters, mainly Mozart's, and reproduced in italics. Around those historical facts, Welsh has woven a tale. Librarians would probably classify it as a historical novel, but it could also be called a fictional biography or imaginative memoirs.

Welsh's tale reveals the hypothesized psyche of the protagonist, the subjective side that does not go down in history. Whereas the facts are biographical, the feelings are, one might say, autobiographical. The book relates one day in the life of the protagonist, and its interior monologue allows access to unspoken thoughts. On this one day, memory functions to recoup a lifetime. The protagonist tests out her values, as they emerged through the course of life, on the value systems of others with whom she came in contact. Memories of the past, as well as reflections on the present – aging, aloneness, and approaching death – pass through her mind. In that it constitutes a sorting out of priorities, the book is also about youth and about love.

The conversational tone of the work rings true, as

Constanze, conscious of her 'simplicity,' talks with herself and an interlocutor, her sister Sophie. Topics range from food to childhood to love and beyond. Early in her reflections, Constanze realizes that conversation deals only with surface matters, and "it was really about something else" (44). It is the abyss beneath the talk –between the lines – that lends it such an enigmatic quality. "Were you ever happy, really happy?" (58). The answer, it turns out, is a mere "twice for five minutes" (59). Is that enough for a lifetime? The question is raised, but it obviously admits of no answer. Or, from another context: "It had to be enough" (106). Happiness is often associated with love; but "Who even knows what love is, and what only confusion, youth, and infatuation?" (48).

Happiness, at least for an eighteenth-century woman, was thought to inhere in marriage, and Constanze feels forced to defend her marriage to herself, as well as to the outside world. She reflects on her life together with Mozart and their conjugal bliss. Constanze was no prude, and she talks about sexuality as frankly as an eighteenth-century woman could. If that is not openly enough, Welsh cites from Mozart's letters, for he was never known to mince words. Constanze also remembers the alleged extra-marital affairs on both sides; and she reacts with jealously at her husband's "peccadillos," while attempting to justify her own alleged dalliance. Some of that was serious, and the couple had periodic rows. But none of that matters anymore, and the Papageno/Pamina duet from *The Magic Flute* stands, for her, as symbol of their happiness together.

But does the outside world really not matter? Constanze is still smarting under the Mozart family's rejection of her. According to Mozart's father, she was "not the right girl" for the great man, although for Mozart, as revealed in his letters, she was always his "dearest little wife" and "Stanzi Marini." Yet the rejection by his family was life-long, and it still, even after all these years, puts her on the defensive. Looking at a portrait of Mozart's late sister, Nannerl, Constanze muses about the later years: "We were two old women in a small town; two old women, both alone, both still – or again, after all these years – circling around one man, whom you knew at the piano and I knew in bed. Excuse me, Nannerl, but that's how it was" (48). Constanze views Nannerl as the "obedient daughter," who, unlike her famous brother, internalized the class consciousness of a society that excluded "a Weber woman." But her sister reminds her: "Don't get excited, Constanze. It's over. They're all dead" (62). And one believes to hear Mozart's *Requiem* in the background.

Did Constanze understand her husband's music? Or, more to the point, who does 'understand' Mozart's music? Constanze had grown up in a musical family, which was not unusual for the time and place. Her father had taught her to play the piano, and her older sister was an opera singer. Mozart had "explained to her how he transformed powerful feelings into music" (18). But she was young, hardly twenty years old when they married, and no genius. It was late in life, Constanze realizes, when she learned "to think." But, she excuses herself, how was a young woman supposed to learn to think critically when there were so few choices? "She liked his music; but it was the man, not the music that she loved, the man who made her laugh" (11). The laughter, Constanze reflects, and "the sensuality belonged to him, just as his music belonged to him. He was no pure spirit. Do you think that a pure spirit could have written those operas?"

The sisters are fond of humming operatic melodies, from *Don Giovanni* to *Figaro*. The latter leads Constanze to recall Mozart's resistance to authority. Rumblings of the French Revolution are heard in the background, and she reviews the ideals of *liberté, égalité, fraternité*. But that too seems long ago, and meanwhile the railroad has come in. "Imagine if they had had a train fifty years ago. Then they probably would have brought the revolution here too ... and you wouldn't be safe anywhere" (63). Matches, whereby "nowadays any child can light a fire" (52), was another recent invention at the time. But the past is more real than the present. The young couple's married life, from 1782 to 1791, though plagued by financial difficulties, was the time when Mozart composed his greatest works. Yet Mozart went unrecognized in his time and died in virtual poverty.

"Recognition is a powerful beauty treatment" (37), and helpful also for self-esteem. Constanze, to the extent that she was regarded at all, was always and only the widow of Mozart. The recognition she received later in life from numerous Mozart-admirers was certainly reassuring to her; but the visitors who came sought in her the shadow of him. Even her second husband, the Danish diplomat Nissen, sought primarily contact with the genius. "The affection that he showed her was actually always directed toward him too, the dead man. He was the one Nissen was looking for, even in her arms" (29). Constanze became the administrator of the estate after Nissen's death, and she basks in a feeling of accomplishment and a sense of affluence. Perhaps her smugness is petty; but what in life is not 'petty' in retrospect?

Her thoughts revert to childhood, the formative time for each of us; and childhood, with all its thrills, is vividly present. Constanze thinks with fondness of her father, but with antipathy toward her mother, who was allegedly a difficult person. As Tolstoy wrote in *Anna Karenina*: "All happy families resemble one another, but each unhappy family is unhappy in its own way." The adult carries something of the child within her, and Constanze feels compelled to justify her likes and dislikes, if only to herself. Her siblings comprised three sisters, with the relationships characterized by the usual sibling rivalry. That was especially apparent with her older sister Aloysia, "Louise," who had a beautiful singing voice and with whom Mozart first fell in love. Was Constanze a second choice? The question presents itself, but she, like each of us on the defensive, has to answer it in the negative.

She also thinks of her own children. If Mozart biographies chronicle the dates of his musical compositions, Constanze's 'biography' is punctuated by pregnancies and child-bearing. Mozart and Constanze had six children, only two of whom survived to adulthood. "The children died ... no one knew why, and once again a little casket was carried out" (103). Carl became a diplomat and Wolfgang, "Wowi," a musician; but they stood in the shadow of their famous father: "The sons would remain sons ... always only sons ... and the worst thing was that they knew it" (42). She thinks of the distance between herself and her sons, both empirically and emotionally, and realizes, "that children are no defense against loneliness" (35).

Age, of course, entails the past, and the nature and strangeness of memory is itself topicalized: "The days and the years ran together" (37), and "memories do not remain fixed" (53). As the shadows grow denser, the memories, as preserved in objects, press in. In hindsight, one has the desire to change the past, and "everything could have been entirely different" (70). But said is said and done is done. "The mind could, however, bend the memories into place, bend them carefully as a goldsmith bends an ornament. Thus one could gradually get the things into a shape that did not hurt so much" (90). That is largely what Constanze does on this day, as she "examines her life as if it were a ledger" (104).

But there is also another way of dealing with the past. "Alternatively, one could close the door and turn the key twice in the lock. Not think about it anymore" (90). That was what Constanze had done with her emotions surrounding Mozart's death. Mourning was, of course, appropriate and socially acceptable; but anger was not. In a late-night fit of anger, which forms the climax of the book, Constanze experiences emotions that

she had repressed for fifty years. "He had left her, had
simply sneaked off into death and left her alone and
helpless" (92). The reader might beg 'special pleading' for
the dead one, especially if he is a musical genius; but
emotions, by definition, are not rational, they simply *are*.
"A fifty-year-old helpless rage burned in her throat" (94),
as the pent-up emotions come to the surface. The tears
have a cathartic effect, and Constanze awakens the next
morning with a new zeal for life.

Depression, as is known today, often results from a
sense of powerlessness. In this case, it was probably the
lack of power fifty years earlier that troubled her so
deeply that she could not admit it, even to herself, until
the problem had been overcome. One is reminded of
Christine Brückner's book, *Desdemona – If You Had
Only Spoken!*, which fictively presents "eleven uncen-
sored speeches of eleven incensed women." They are the
consorts of famous men, such as Petrarch, Luther, and
Goethe. Like Constanze Mozart, the women were virtually invisible in their lifetime and never had a chance to
have their say. The enforced silence through history
leads, in Brückner's imaginative account, to anger and an
urgent need, now at last, to speak out. "A voice of one's
own," in the contemporary phrase, is a prerequisite for
empowerment, that is, for well-being.

Yet, life leads to death. Alternately dimly and
acutely, a person is aware of declining strength and "the
thousand other changes that so softly and impreceptibly
creep over one" (74). Constanze senses an increasing
aloneness: "With each year there were fewer people who

shared the past with her, and with each death notice the past became more brittle. Each death left behind a hole, through which a cold wind forced its way into the present. Present – what was that?" (83). Mozart's death – his presentiments of death, her helplessness, and the reactions of others – is relived. The fear of death looms constantly in the background, and the coldness and emptiness lend a sense of anxiety to the whole. "It was not death that she feared but rather dying" (84), which leads to the prayer: "Holy Virgin ... don't let me die alone" (88). Unmitigated fear alternates with the desire to live, "to live with a passion that she herself did not understand" (84).

Welsh guides the reader through the scala of emotions, from the dread of death to the will to live, from the joys and sorrows of youth to the selfhood of maturity and the fragility of old age. That lets the reader participate in a deeply personal way in thoughts and feelings that we all know but that often go unspoken. Welsh is never patronizing toward her protagonist, nor does she attempt to eulogize her; rather, she takes Constanze seriously and respects her for what she is. By projecting the individual life onto the dimension of general human experience, Welsh is able to offer a text that is larger than the persona portrayed. However distanced from or empathetic with the protagonist the reader may feel, by being privy to this private sphere, one is able to glean insight into the movement of emotions.

Welsh's way has a great appeal. It is the way neither of a fantasy nor of an ideal, but rather the way of the world as it is for a lot of people. Each of us wants to be regarded for the person he or she is – not only as spouse, parent, child, or friend of a famous person, but as oneself. If by 'important' is meant an accomplishment that outlives its creator, Constanze, like most of us, has none. But if by 'important' is meant life itself, we, the readers, can benefit from Constanze's reflections on life. It is superfluous to point to her weaknesses, of which there were many. Welsh recognizes that there is plenty of guilt to go around for everyone. But what does one do with it? The emphasis is on the psychic mechanisms that we all use to justify our behavior to ourselves and the world. The book can be regarded as a portrait of human strength and frailty.

Renate Welsh is well known for her books about what might be called 'emotional intelligence.' Born in Vienna in 1937, Welsh is a leading author in Austria today in the area of children's and young-adult literature. Anyone who supposes that "kiddy lit" is a simplified or less valuable form is literature is certainly mistaken. To be sure, it does not deal with the abstractions of philosophical systems; but it does include large areas of psychology, sociology, and linguistics, certainly also politics, religion, and gender issues – in short, all the material and spiritual components that make up our lives. Welsh, in her poetological essays entitled *Stories behind the Stories*, writes about the human need "to make room for feelings, room where perhaps a deep breath is possible."

That is as necessary for adults as it is for children, and Welsh's books for adults deal with some of the same issues: self and other, isolation and integration, identity and self-esteem, and the desire to be loved and respected. Adult fears are often carry-overs from childhood; and the goal, at any age, is to learn better to deal not only with the problems but also with one's emotions. For example, Welsh wrote another documentary novel about a nineteenth-century woman, *Das Lufthaus* (1994; House of Cards). It deals with emigration from Austria to "Amerika"; and with the familial and societal pressures that led, in that historical case, to the woman's insanity. Interpersonal affairs certainly include some of the most difficult aspects of life – but, on this account, also the most rewarding. Welsh demonstrates the complexity and richness of human relations.

Constanze Mozart opens with the protagonist's thoughts about a statue that is being erected to honor her late husband. A later ironic reflection in that regard applies self-referentially also to the text itself: The text/statue, "like all images, would tell more about the one who created it than about the one it represented" (106). In that spirit it is at once Renate Welsh/Constanze Mozart who says: "Only live" (84).